AGILE PROJECT MANAGEMENT

A Complete Beginner's Guide to Agile Project Management

Marcus Ries & Diana Summers

Table of Contents

Introduction

Of all the strategies used to develop software related to project management, Agile provides enough options for project managers and software developers alike for exploiting a wide range of incorporated methodologies. These methodologies are either adaptation of a system in vogue before Agile came into existence or have been developed by modern exponents in more recent times.

Business management solutions have always depended on customary values derived from progressive trial and error. Though this book will tell you in detail all you need to know about developing and implementing business development software and management, it does not purport to be an exhaustive analysis. And, you will learn more by implementing and interacting with your colleagues, in conjunction with what you learn within the pages of the book.

Chapter 1: Principles of the Adaptive Project Framework

Experience Teaches Best

It is possible to improve management practices relating to policies by enhancing decisions on a continuing basis through the use of a structured and systematic process with outcomes that are, in turn, a consequence of earlier decisions. This is termed "Adaptive" management. So, we understand 'learning by doing' is adaptive (Sadahisa Kato, Jack Ahem, IDEAS Home, Taylor & Francis Journals, Journal of Environmental Planning and Management, Volume 51, 2008, Issue 4) to the extent that we understand the consequence of our actions and can grow from those experiences.

This idea was brought to the forefront in ecological studies that focused on the survival rate of fish in an ecosystem that was continually being subject to change. Carl J. Walters and his fellow ecologist, C. S. Holling, used the concept of adaptive management to understand and implement this framework of learning, derived from previous decisions and consequences and outcomes.

This structured process of improving management policies was subsequently implemented in various projects including those used in the management of the Grand Canyon National Park and Everglades. (*Lev Virine, PM Times, Friday 02, May 2008 04:51*)

Iterative Learning Process

It resembles the Agile Project Management system in two ways.

- Focus is on the organizational aspect is adaptive. This means the iterative judgment structure depended upon decisions made earlier on and their consequences.
- Irreversibility in making judgments was circumvented at all costs. This means that the system incorporated flexibility in strategy at all levels of operation.

In certain ways, the adaptive administration procedure varied and included more details that helped study and improve the process. The inclusion of quantitative investigation systems that impacted actual project performances helped in arriving at more efficient choices.

- Proposition testing by analyzing many models side by side

- Quantitative analysis of the project risk

- Measurement of actual values

In short, project management is undertaken based on the outcome of results obtained for previous deployments of the same idea.

Learning Curve Is Tough for Many

Traditional project management techniques continue to be the scourge for many managers. Nevertheless, numerous software companies and business houses have embraced the "Agile" principles for dealing with management problems. It is worth noting that compared to animals, birds and fish, the human psyche seems to be very resilient to change. Humans adapt at a much slower rate.

The reason for this lies in the way the social fabric of society is put together. All people want consistency in approach. So, they tend to question any change. Since birds and animals do not possess this reasoning power, they make the change and adapt much quicker than humans are able to.

For humans, a pre-determined course of action is preferable. It is not a good management principle to take another course of action when you already have a plan of action. This in short is the Sunk Cost Effect.

A View of the Sunk Cost Effect

People tend to continue working on a lost cause simply because they reason that it is worthwhile continuing something in which they have put in any kind of investment or effort. (*Arkes and Blumer*, 1985). The onus is on the person to project him or herself as one who does not waste. The psychology needs to be understood because of the significance it has in that the sunk cost effect cannot be explained or categorized under known theories on social psychology. In addition, having knowledge of economics does not lessen this effect.

You can cover all aspects of your management structure with new policies but you will invariably find some old ideology or some old managerial aspect remaining within the new methodology. As mentioned previously, the number of organizations that desire a complete makeover from traditional Gantt Charts and established management techniques to the new "Agile" system where you begin to change everything that is old is less than a handful.

Elements of a Project

From the viewpoint of traditional project managers, elements of a project would include risk, complexity, duration and cost. And the project variables would comprise of client involvement, business value, goal and solution clarity and lastly market stability.

In a post by Rick Freedman in TechRepublic June 22, 2010, we see Robert Wysocki compare management techniques to that of cooking skills a chef has based on the recipes he or she has at hand. He highlights the Adaptive Framework by outlining the boundary conditions that exist between a traditional system of approach and the Agile Management Framework.

Adaptive Approach to Traditional Approach

Project Management Office policies for Project Managers have their basis on development lifecycles that remain constant. Adhering to standard methods, these managers deliver consistent results, as long the external Framework is defined. Adaptive Project Managers do not have a specific goal in sight. They must rely on iterative feedback to toil their way towards the theoretical result. These results from the Framework are recognizable as such from previous instances as:

- Change drives you forward

- Client involvement is deep and imperative

- Client makes a tangible difference

- Discovery method is iterative and depends on the method of delivery

Chapter 2: Learning Agile Software Development Techniques

In this chapter, we will see what Agile Software Development is and how it plays an important role in modern software management techniques. The biggest challenge in Agile Software Development is to maintain the synchrony between the stability existing among adaptive groups (meaning the team and all stakeholders), the ongoing feedback (from each Sprint) and the team effort. Doing this helps safeguard deployable yields that are aptly attuned to dynamic requests. Unceasing evaluation and testing with iterative forecasting guarantees augmented group possession and healthier interaction.

At the beginning, in 2001, the publication of the Agile Manifesto unified the various software practices (This is discussed in detail in the next chapter). *Manifesto for Agile Software Development* was formulated by 17 software developers who met in Utah. Creator of the Adaptive Software Development, Jim Highsmith, defended the coming together of technologies like XP, DSDM, Crystal Clear and Scrum and called for a balance between all related developments. But now, let us look at the 'what' and 'how' of Agile

Delimiting the Process

First, we have the team. The team, as specified by Agile, would be comprised of closely-knit units. Each one of these units – the customer, project management, quality assurance and developers – interact frequently. Deliveries are the end result of the work that is determined by parameters known as dependencies. Daily assessment of dependencies and work targets make the deliveries extremely short-term.

These are referred to as Sprints. The delivery cycle will not be more than 3 – 4 weeks for each Sprint. Project teams in Agile follow communication methods that are direct and open. This helps everyone develop an instant understanding of the needs and goals of the client. Further planning and delivery, alongside deployment of software, are shaped based on this recommendation.

Scope of Management in an Agile Project

In Agile, all management decision responsibility will rest with the Project Manager. This will determine - to a large extent - what direction the entire team will take. Every person in the team will be escalated to the role of the Project Manager when the situation warrants, provided he or she has the needed skills.

Actions Initiated by the Project Manager

- An Agile Project Manager has all of the duties mentioned below. In addition, certain duties may be added or deleted depending on what the project is.

- Aids team members to create adequate functionality in their software based on the log of requirements given to them.

- Coordinates implementation of Agile values in the project Framework.

- Augments tools and routines that the development crew comes up with for the project.

- Makes communications better and smoother to help improve the effectiveness of delivery.

- In his or her core capacity, the Manager will get rid of any impediments that exist within the project Framework.

- As the mentor, the Agile project manager keeps the team motivated.

- Getting the team together regularly for meeting and discussing problems and solutions of an immediate nature.

Now let us examine what the Agile network is. This helps us get to understand its functionality better.

Actions that are not within the scope of the Agile network

Management does not place any restrictions or demands on the team responsible for software development. Further, they do not give any particular task to any member of the project team. They will abide by the informed decisions taken by team members and will not go against these decisions.

Management cannot and will not make decisions on behalf of the team or team members. They will not issue directives to team members or ask them to perform tasks. They will take no part in originating Product policy and any related procedural judgments.

Actions that you can expect will take place

For all developments and events, the team members will go by common sense ruling over written rules. They share the responsibility of building up to the overall action of the team project manager. These will also incorporate adequate motivating and directing skills for their fellow team members. The spirit of togetherness and 'go-get' attitude is a continuous ongoing thing and not just a slogan.

Implementation of management decisions thus gets executed faster. Progress is made without any delay since they do not wait for any 'boss' to tell them what to do. Software development proceeds unhindered and resource flow is speedy.

Chapter 3: Agile Manifesto

Agile Manifesto is the basis for all Agile related developments. The four values of the Agile manifesto, as given by Holling, Walters, et al., will be the priority list:

- Value is more for the interactions and interacting team members than that given for tools and processes.

- Getting the work done is only secondary to the needs of the client.

- Written words are guides but software that works and collaboration dominate.

- Sticking to an idea is good, but change is better.

Features of Agile Project Management

We can gather the salient points of Agile Project Management as the *ten principles* relating to the four values given in the Agile manifesto:

1. At all times, the team retains the power to implement processes and plans

2. Always go through small increments of development, iterate from the results

3. Use 80/20 rule effectively (Complete the 20% that is going to impact your rest 80% work in the best way possible first – Pareto's law)

4. User or client must have full interaction with the ongoing process at every stage

5. Keep the requirements in sight always. This way they remain current. Understanding of the requirement is at a high level so that good anticipation of needs is present.

6. It is imperative to finish each step completely before moving on to the next.

7. The effort is a result of the collaboration of all stakeholders at every level. This keeps the feedback alive and progresses vibrant.

8. Requirements will change and are expected but the timescale does not change.

9. Frequent delivery of the Product is a top priority

10. Tests take place frequently; tests are integral to the lifecycle of the project.

Basic Strategy of Agile

When you are standing in the checkout aisle in the department store, the last thing you want to see is for the salesperson to close the aisle. Strictness in formulating any action plan will result in inordinate delays due to unavoidable changes in the plan of action. If management was just about to order a dozen eggs and get them delivered in time, you would probably be able to conduct a dozen negotiations a day and subsequently become wealthy. But most plans are susceptible to failure. Indeed, the wise man foresees the failure and makes provisions for this. That, in a nutshell, is Agile.

Adapting for Change

Incremental changes towards the attainment of the goal -- like the sun in the morning sky, the sales page begins with a blank and begins to fill up. Along with that, you have the scope for a change! Agile is not about success alone, it is about arriving at the point of success. To succeed, you need to be adaptable (we will talk about that in a moment) and be ready for changes. To keep those changes small, we need to split up the time plan into small digestible bits.

Every time the external situation changes, you are bound to make a deviation from your original plan. This increases the chances of failure for your project! And the longer the duration of your project, the more is the risk of change is involved. When you keep the intervals small, there is every chance for correction. Moreover, the deviation will be small and this can be corrected easily!

Keep in Touch Always

Agile keeps accent on one more aspect -- interaction with the client. Why this is important will be obvious in a moment. Assuming that you are the type who is willing to take changes in your stride, you can stand the stormy weather and you will perform well in the sunshine too -- we call this adaptable. You need to know what you are going to adapt to. Kaput! Simple, you are going to *adapt to the wishes* of your customer.

But how are you going to do that? By keeping in constant touch with him. Eureka! So, this then is the final principle of Agile. You must be in constant interaction with the client. If he wants a pink egg, color your egg pink.

- Small changes that you can fit into your stride

- Be adaptable

- Keep in touch with your client

Healthy Growth at the Workplace

You will thus develop a strong working atmosphere where there is a healthy flow of information. You will get your customers to sail along with you on your trip to attain your goal. This type of close interaction will ensure that you meet all the needs of the client. Individual employees are taught to 'inspect and adapt' -- a precise method of learning the skills of the trade (*The Agile Movement*, agilemethodology.org). Most of the software used lays emphasis on a short work plan and quick results instead of loads of notes and instructions and fewer results.

On a comparative basis, Agile Project Management manages to cut down on non-essential communications and bridge the gap to the requirements of the client effectively. This is done essentially by the Agile system, which does not tolerate inordinate delays in communication or elaborations in the procedure. Frequent testing helps the Agile operators to take frequent notes and make corrections according to the wishes of the client. This helps the process move faster and with more efficiency.

Chapter 4: Dynamic System Development Model (DSDM)

DSDM Methodology for Management of Business

DSDM is used for formulation of software designing techniques using Agile Project Management. The latest version of the Dynamic System Development Model (DSDM) is the DSDM Atern. The name is a short form for Arctic Tern -- a bird that is renowned for its adaptation and collaboration. This approach has proven successful for software and non-software projects.

The controlled process has enough flexibility to deliver solutions that fit into tight delivery timescales. Techniques such as modelling and iterative development merge admirably through the appropriate use of knowledge. You can market the business solutions within months - if not weeks – from the beginning of the project.

Adaptation is Simple with Atern

Atern process was created to bind business processes and strategies, office automation and technology including communications, around the people core comprising of staff and organization along with their skills to provide a development process that is simple to deploy and use. It does not rely on any vendor but helps enable people improve their capabilities by enhancing a tool and methodology independent approach.

So, while nothing is built perfectly the first time, most of the solution - up to 80% - can be discovered in 20% of the time needed to create the whole answer, which is the Pareto principle (Kelly Walters, 15 April, 2007 |*10 Key Principles of Agile Development*). By contrast, in the sequential approach, the subsequent step will only be initiated when the present one has been completed.

The Seven Phases of the Atern Project

Unlike software-oriented methodologies like Scrum, Atern takes into account the entire lifecycle of the project. The incorporated disciplines of project management give due consideration to feasibility of the suggested results, perfect setting up of devices that guarantee the project profits and also confirm that fundamental working methods are in place before initiation of in-depth work.

Pre-Project Phase: In this phase, there is an agreement to the terms. The project gets initiated. This can be said to be the 'zero' point of the project.

Feasibility Studies: This is the justification phase where the linearity of progress is studied. This does not consume much of the project timeline. The business case is outlined. The viability is declared.

Establishing Foundations: This phase occurs before the development work gets underway, when technical mechanisms and operation standards are agreed upon. A high range of operation for the base is established through proper comprehension and analysis of the key aspects of the project.

Exploration stage: This is the beginning of the iterative phase where various models are explored. New directions are analyzed and compromises are made if there is less chance of success. Functionality is not limited and the high level of expectation is maintained as a driving factor.

Engineering Phase: In this phase, the solution undergoes deployment studies. Models are tested to ensure the final product is deliverable.

Deployment Phase: This is the phase when the final solution is put into place. The final check of the requirements is checked and ticked off. The project becomes ready for handing over to the client.

Post-Project Phase: This is the follow-through phase when the client has possessed the final solution. The team ensures the smooth working of the entire project for several lifecycles. Any fine-tuning needed is done as and where required.

Chapter 5: Principles that Guide the DSDM Atern Team

We see these features in DSDM:

- Delivery of the basic functionality is fast; more features and working solutions being supplied at consistent intervals. Regular workshops and prototyping, presentations, and daily standups help to maintain the interaction levels.

- Every user can bring a new direction to the progress of the project; collaboration in the spirit of shared ownership helps improve the input. Eliminates the bureaucratic red tape.

- System will deliver the project result in time and inside the budget allocated; dates are kept constant.

- Bringing users in close contact with the development makes them one with the project; they are unlikely to abandon the product being fashioned and are more likely to adopt it. Users keep giving their opinion and views on how the end result is shaping; constant input will increase the adherence to the true purpose of the output.

- Incremental development of the product is tested constantly. This eliminates the risk of a wrong development.

- You can get an early appraisal of the success (or failure) of the project; you will not have to wait until the project is halfway through to find out. This iterative building and testing helps to achieve a good quality.

- Every development is openly visible and direct; a well-defined business case helps the system deliver priorities as required. Product viability is kept in sight throughout the duration of the project.

- Standard of the output is fixed at the outset. This quality is maintained throughout.

Core Techniques to Use in this Methodology

Modelling: This is the diagrammatic visualization of the aspects of the solution that is being worked out. This is needed to develop a better understanding of the whole process and the method that is employed to arrive at the final solution. Team members are able to participate freely in the discussions about the project and thus contribute better to the solution.

Testing: This is one of the top priorities in DSDM. Every iteration will undergo testing, as this is the way to assure quality in the final product. You will find plenty of liberty in choosing the testing method for management since it is not tool or technique specific.

MoSCoW: This is how you prioritize items in DSDM. It is an acronym that tells us this:

MUST -- The needed minimum standard to be able to qualify for the business in hand.

SHOULD -- This requirement is to be met; it is needed for the value of the product greatly.

COULD -- This is an extra qualification that would be desirable.

WON'T -- These things will certainly not be considered and so are not desirable in the product.

Configuration Management: This is the method of dealing with changes in a systematic manner. This technique helps us to maintain the system without it losing its integral value for a long time. Configuration Management is useful for iterative processes where changes are mediated at a rapid pace over a relatively short span of time.

Workshop: All stakeholders gather at the Workshop and conduct discussions. They develop a better understanding of the requirements and functionalities involved. This is one of the most significant methods of DSDM. It helps foster understanding.

Prototyping: This is most useful for early detection of flaws and shortcomings within the system or product. Prototyping consists of creating models that are representative of the final product in all its aspects. Test-driving by future users helps them to discover the features that they want or do not want to incorporate. It contributes to the huge success factor of DSDM.

Time boxing: This is one of the development methodologies of DSDM. While developing an IS on time, time-boxing helps to break up the project into sizable chunks so that each is controlled and ordered according to the situation. The requirements for each portion are determined according to the MoSCoW principle. When time or money is a priority, items with low priority are omitted. However, making sure that 20% of the most important material is already assembled will ensure that you have a fully assembled product ready for delivery according to the Pareto principle.

Atern Helps Eliminate the Following Problems

Late Delivery: Every increment is time fixed. Since the events are all time-boxed, the problem of late delivery never occurs. If you fix the date of a delivery of a product in the Atern framework, then it will be delivered on time.

Building the Right Thing -- the Business Changing Their Mind: You involve the client in the Atern framework right from the beginning. The business house approves each increment every step of the way. This eliminates the chances of the client changing their mind midway through the project.

Communication Problem: This problem never arises. The entire framework is built on a well-knit communication network. The system becomes efficient when there is an improvement in the communication channels.

Unused Features: Since there is project appraisal at each incremental stage, and the client will be constantly voicing their opinion regarding the features of the product, the chances of any of the features being 'unworthy' does not happen. If the client does not like something it is removed in that increment itself.

Over-engineering: This is present at the other end of the scale. Just as before, there is no possibility that the product will have any extra features. All the progress in every stage is reported to the all stakeholders and the clients. They will tell their opinion at each stage and if there is anything extraneous in their sight, then that will be removed in that increment.

Delivered Solution is Not What the Business Wanted: The chance that the whole project is going the wrong way is not possible. The entire framework develops in increments. This means that if there is any deviation from the product that the client has in mind, it will be brought to the attention of the Solution Development Team in that increment itself. Thereby, a correction is made at that stage and the possibility of error is eliminated.

Delayed Return on Investment: Efficient handling of the business end of the DSDM project ensures that the market value of the product is appreciable. The timely delivery of the product further enhances its market value. Return on investment is therefore guaranteed to be good and timely.

Chapter 6: Different Roles in DSDM

The roles in the project are three-fold. First, we have the *Project Roles* where you see five people coming together. The dominant role is that of the Team Leader who also monitors the functions of the *Solution Development Roles*. In the Project Roles, he reports to the Project Manager and interacts with the Business Sponsor, the Technical Coordinator and the Business Visionary.

In the Solution Development Role, you will find there is a Business Advisor together with the Solution Tester and Solution Developer. They will work with the Team Leader and are advised by the Business Ambassador. In the *Other Roles*, we have three people. The Workshop Facilitator and the Atern Coach are regulars. The third person, the specialist, may be required for some projects alone. A Scribe is a person who keeps the record of all discussions and meetings.

Project roles

Dual Role of the Team Leader: The Team Leader is the head and participates in both the Project Role and the Solution Development Role. The Team Leader works with the Project Manager. His duty will include the supervision of the working of the Solution Development Team so that they are adhering to the details of the plan and remaining as one cohesive unit. This leadership role will be filled by the most apt person (who in that situation may be Solution Developer, or Business Analyst) and will last for the duration until the team is through to the next stage. This role could be time-boxed to the same person too, depending on the focus.

Duties primarily are to ensure that the review and testing activity is done in the best possible manner. He keeps reporting the progress to the Project Manager. He keeps focus on the iterative development so that the process is adequately controlled. All the team activities come under his scrutiny so that progress is maintained. He gets the team pointed towards the ultimate delivery of the products agreed upon in a timely manner. He rises up in his role to that of Technical Coordinator or Project Manager if required to deal with the risks and related issues at the level of the Development Time-box. He presides over the team meetings conducted every day and ensures that they are brief, focused and timely.

Executive Sponsor: Also known as the Business Sponsor, this role is a high-ranking appointment and he or she remains on the job for the complete period of the project. He has the entire accountability for the Business Case, including the returns and reimbursements once the resolution of the work is provided. His duty is to guarantee smooth appreciation, fast advancement with greatest commitment to supplying the anticipated solution for the project. His (or her) rank empowers the individual to force open barred accesses, decide on commercial matters and press onward with monetary judgements.

He makes finance obtainable for the project and maintains the Business Case, checks to confirm that it is possible to go ahead with the project in line with the Business Case, creates rapid reply for intensified problems.

Project Manager: He takes the entire responsibility for the complete solution delivery. Albeit, his role is not fixed at any particular place in the project framework, he ensures technical and business aspects of the delivery and is present right through from the foundation establishment to the solution deployment.

His duties will entail keeping track of progress as per the plan projections, keeping the team motivated to attaining their objectives, tackling problems that arise from the solution development team, high-level detailing of schedule and project (this does not include task planning), making sure the configurations of the project remain correct, arranging for specialists roles whenever required, maintaining frequent communication with top brass of management and government authorities, handling issues that project risk and taking the appropriate technical or business role to solve the risk, handling the business side for the Solution Development Team, and giving tips and guidance to Solution Development Team when needed. He configures the project and ensures resource availability, manages escalated issues and takes care of risks.

Business Visionary: This high-ranking station is a part that vigorously contributes to the Business Sponsor. He keeps updating the Business Case through interactive effort with the team and getting particulars of the work to be completed from the Business Sponsor. He delivers tactical information and is involved for the whole period of the development. He safeguards the benefits described according to the Business Case, acquired as and when the resolution is brought about.

He (or she) shares in all meetings both appraisal and design, checks the important requirements, remains as the symbol of the business vision, assists in realizing this vision as practical work, will approve modifications desirable for the Prioritized Requirements List, aids to spread the idea to parties who express interest, is the absolute authority for all quarrels, safeguards teamwork among the stakeholders, monitors plan advancement in line with the Business Vision, and guarantees resources are obtainable for the business when necessary.

Technical coordinator: This design authority helps the Solution Development Team achieve the perfect answer all the time. This person has the task of maintaining the quality of production through technical cohesion and advises on all matters of innovations. He will help the team to remain united in their approach to making the delivery.

His (or her) responsibilities will include identifying with all manner of technical and architectural details and risks. His role will be to escalate problems to the Project Manager if the situation warrants it. His word for the final solution is revered since he checks the technical details. His acceptance of the architectural technicalities and details will begin at the start of the project. He then checks for non-architectural needs and establishes a working method for obtaining the solution. He helps realize the conversion of the technicalities in real time. He will also establish the working environment that is suitable for the specifications. Lastly, he will check the work progress to see that the quality of the work is up to the specified levels.

Solution development team

Business Ambassador: This role will be within the scope of the Solution Development Team in the business category. Business Ambassador (as this person is otherwise known) will provide business details to those who are going to be using it. He or she will develop and implement the perspectives suitable for and relating to the business aspect of the product being delivered by the DSDM framework. The link between the project and the business on a routine basis is operated and enhanced by the skills of this Ambassador. He or she uses the knowledge and possesses the authority to ensure that the correct solution regarding the business emerges. This is brought about by the desire that the person has and the way they use the knowledge to enhance the business end of the bargain. There is no seniority associated with this position, merely the allocation of time and responsibility to help the person take the right decisions.

The Ambassador will work to provide, on a daily basis, the report that the correct solution is being arrived at, and that user training is being imparted. He or she provides the business viewpoint of project decisions, while systematically testing solutions by organizing and controlling them properly. The Ambassador will necessarily attend all daily meetings. For testing solutions, he or she will provide the specifics of the business. He will develop the document for the business user for the final solution.

Solution Developer: The Solution Developer works with the team on a full-time basis. All the functional and nonfunctional requirements are brought to fulfillment from the interpretation stage of the business requirement. If the Solution Developer is not available on a full-time basis, the time-boxing will have to be adjusted in such a manner as to facilitate smooth progress of work. In such situations, the Project Manager will be on hand to handle the risk factor.

On an active working front, the Solution Developer will work to create a deployable solution. This work will proceed on an incremental basis. Models will be developed for deploying the solution correctly in a controlled manner. He will work towards making the documents and models for the final product. This person will record details of technical limitations as per System Definition Architecture. He will test the work before approving its use for the team. He will work out the details of the changes that may be required while reworking the solution or model. Lastly, he will work to assure that the quality is as per the specifications of the work order.

Solution Tester: This role is a full time one. It is integrated into the Solution Development Team. The Technical Testing Strategy will form the basis for the work of the Solution Tester.

He works to evolve solutions for various business test scenarios. On the technical side, he creates and tests cases and reports the results to the Technical Coordinator. These results are studied for Quality Assurance purposes. He helps the Business Advisor and the Business Ambassador in their plan and work of testing in all areas of the work. He reports all findings to the Team Leader in a routine manner.

Business Analyst: This role is integral to the Solution Development Team environment. They help analyze the link between the technical and business aspects of the project. Decisive direction and accurate implementation on a daily basis is vital to the wellbeing of the team. In addition, he assures that the solution generated needs will be implementable and acceptable. For all this, the Business Analyst evolves the methodology required. He is not present in the role of an intermediate link between Business Ambassador, Advisor, and Developers but as the governing and motivating process that enhances better communication and understanding of the environment.

Duties primarily will be in ensuring timely communication of elements of the project on both the business and technical side. He clarifies details and manages the documentation. He develops and distributes the baseline approval for the product. Takes care of the business requirements and provides proper interpretation. Helps supplement the business methodology in a supportive manner for the entire team.

Business Advisor: Of a senior rank, the Business Advisor is called on to assist the Business Ambassador. His specialist input will be of immense benefit when assessing the product in the development and testing stage. He will not necessarily be an intended user and may only be passing advice on the legal or technical details of the business aspect.

He is involved in daily business dealings and decisions. He primarily arranges for the business acceptance testing of solutions for systemizing and controlling the commercial side of the project. He points out the necessary projections of the product that are needed to enhance its market value. He assists in creating the ambient atmosphere for the conduct of testing and getting the marketing side approved. The business user documentation is prepared for developing the business further. He helps to check all the various business contingencies and market situations that could arise for the product being developed. He devises solutions for the same.

Other roles

Atern Coach: This role is especially useful when the team has limited experience in Atern methodology. The person taking up this role must be an Atern expert having suitable experience in guiding teams to achieve goals. The Atern Coach must be capable enough to recognize the two ways to address problems that arise. One is that he could either change the Atern technique, or two, change the external factors under which the technique operates. The DSDM expert will be adept at solving such problems and guiding the team.

Primarily helps in deploying Atern methods and practices so that the team remains focused on the goal in hand. If any team member does not understand the technique, the Atern Coach will help that person understand. Uses the Agile approach to implementing the path towards the goal in a collective manner by all the team members. When there are difficult situations or when any one particular member is experiencing difficulty, the Atern Coach will amend the Atern technique so that it becomes employable and comfortable.

Workshop Facilitator: This role is for managing all workshop processes. A Workshop Facilitator will enhance the communications and help with the preparations regarding the Workshop. He is not responsible for the content but merely augments the context. Thus, he remains independent of the outcome one achieves in the Workshop.

The workshop facilitator also details the scope of the Workshop through discussions with the owner. Then he plans the Workshop and helps one understand the subject area. All participants are required to be affirmed as suitable in terms of becoming empowered as well as being knowledgeable. They will be encouraged to become fully prepared and develop a thorough understanding of the objectives of the Workshop. These participants must be prepared to work to help the Workshop move towards its objective. They must further be conversant with all major areas of concern in the Workshop topics. Lastly, they must be prepared to review the work done against the objectives.

Specialist Roles: Every project has special needs. Depending on what the scope of the project is, the need for specialists too will vary. The Specialist's role will be deployed at the insistence of the Project Manager. He will make a study of the requirements and help supplement the Solution Development Team so that they have the full skill set required to carry out the work. If the Team Leader has the needed skills, he can temporarily fill in until a regular person is found for the job. If they are required for the entire duration of the project, they will be added to the Solution Development Team.

Scribe: You also have the Scribe who documents the decisions taken, along with the discussions among the team members. The Scribe also documents the plans.

List of Products for Atern Projects

In the Agile lifecycle, we have deliverables that are specific to the phase where they are created. Deliverables are those things that comprise of the solution itself or help in regulating the process that creates it, or is something that is required for governing the process and its control.

Two kinds of products

The level of corporate skills and governance will decide the products required for the lifecycle of the project. In DSDM, we have two major types of products. One evolves over time while the other is created within the phase of the lifecycle of the product. The first is termed the evolutionary product while the latter is called the milestone product.

Evolutionary Products

Evolutionary products can be spread out over a few phases. Products may be required for the creation of the solution or may be business-oriented in nature. A few may take part in the governance of the project. For instance, *Terms of Reference* is a governance product created within the pre-project phase. Since it does not overlap with other phases, it is a milestone product. Similarly, the *Benefits Assessment* is a milestone product that is created within the post-project phase.

Examples of Evolutionary products are *Delivery Plan* and *Deployment Plan*. *Delivery Plan* begins in the Foundations phase and ends before the Deployment phase. The *Deployment Plan* begins after the Foundations phase in the Exploration and Engineering phases and carries through until the Delivery phase is completed.

Milestone Products

In the Feasibility phase, we have only a few products. Examples are *Outline Plan* and *Feasibility Assessment*. Similarly, we have milestone products in all the phases as follows:

- In Foundations: Business Foundations, Management Foundations, Solutions Foundations.

- In Exploration and Engineering phase: Time box plan, Time box review record, Evolving Solutions.

- In Deployment: Project Review Report, Deployed Solution.

The *Delivery Control Pack* and *Solutions Assurance Pack* span from Exploration and Engineering to Deployment. However, the *Delivery Control Pack* begins at the Foundations phase itself. The *Prioritized Requirements List* will begin likewise in the Foundations phase but terminates well before the Deployment phase begins. These are all evolutionary products.

Chapter 7: Scrum

Scrum, developed by Ken Schwaber and Jeff Sutherland in the 1990s, represents a holistic approach for a development team to deploy a flexible strategy to attain a common goal. Like the scrum in rugby football where players of opposing teams press against each other to gain control over the ball, the members of the team press forward passing the "ball" back and forth until the Product is delivered.

Scrum Framework is intended for adaptive problems having a multifaceted dimension. It delivers the highest conceivable worth to the Product that you want to provide. While being lightweight and simple to comprehend, the intricacies cannot be easily grasped.

Scrum Team

Essentially a process framework and not a building or manufacturing process by itself, Scrum aims at eliminating deficiencies and overcoming obstacles through teamwork. Scrum Framework encompasses Scrum teams, events, artifacts, and rules. Teams have their roles and the individual components have specific roles within the Framework. While you can organize one or more procedures, the efficacy of each will be defined by the Scrum so that you can *evaluate, learn and improve.*

Scrum Teams are cross-functional. More importantly, they are self-organizing in the sense they do not require any orders or instructions from people outside the team to work. The team members are creative and flexible in their work and possess all the skills required for accomplishing the Product Backlog (the final requirements of the Product as dictated by the client).

The nature of Product delivery is iterative while being incremental. This increases the possibility of feedback that the team can use for improving the delivery. There is always a "Done" Product provided on an incremental basis. This ensures that at any stage of the process, you will always have some useful operational Product offered. This keeps productivity on track with improved scope for creativity.

The Workings of Scrum Team

In the Scrum team, the main three components are these:

1. Product Owner

2. Scrum Master

3. Development Team

Product Owner

The Product Owner does three things. One, he maintains the

aspects of the Product Backlog. Two, he maximizes the Product value. And thirdly, he is responsible for the work produced by the Development Team.

While he can employ various methods for raising and sustaining Product value, managing Product Backlog will comprise of these points:

- First and foremost, ensure the transparency and visibility of the Product Backlog so that everyone knows what is expected at any and all points in time.

- The items are listed clearly in the Product Backlog.

- Augment productivity by the Development Team so that value of the work they do is increased.

- Order items in the Product Backlog in such a way as to make the attainment of the goal easier, cheaper and fruitful.

- Make sure the items are clearly understood by each of the members of the Development Team.

This remains the responsibility but not the duty of the Product Owner, in the sense, he might have the Development Team to do it. However, he will answer for it. He is a single person who must be addressed if any change is required in the Product Backlog items. The work orders for the Development Team come only from the Product Owner. His desire is apparent in the list of items arranged in the Product Backlog.

Development Team

This is a set of professionally qualified workers whose primary objective is to ensure the delivery of a working and releasable "Done" product when each Sprint concludes. This is done by the team members in increments. The employing concern gives full powers to the Development Team to organize their work and manage themselves at the workplace. This type of synergy development helps motivate the team and raise it effectiveness and efficiency. They are distinguishable by these characteristics:

- They self-organize and answer to no one – even the Scrum Master cannot tell them what to do or how to make increments for the release of product from the Backlog.

- They exist as a team – they have cross-functionality inbuilt into the team that helps them deliver the increment.

- Individual team members may have special capabilities but they can be spoken of only by the team taken as a whole.

- There will never be any sub-teams within the Development Team, even though you might have separate sections like building or painting.

- All members will have one and the same title of Developer.

There are no exceptions to any of these rules.

Size of the Development Team

From interaction considerations, the size of the team should be bigger than three and smaller than nine in number. The reason is that when you have fewer than two members the interactions become limited. The skill set too is compromised. When the number exceeds nine, the problem of coordination sets in. Interactions become too much and management of different skill sets becomes burdensome. In the normal course, the Scrum Master and the Product Owner remain apart from the team and are not counted as one of the members.

Scrum Master

The only responsibility of the Scrum Master will be to ensure that every team member is acting according to the Scrum guidelines and procedures. His role is that of servant-leader. He helps maximize value by facilitating changes in collaborations. He maintains a perspective on the 'useful' and 'not useful' actions that are done by the team.

Service to the Development Team

Of the many ways the Scrum Master is useful to the Development Team, the important ones are as follows:

- Removes any stumbling blocks in the path of progress of work.

- Helps ensure high value of the product.

- Assists the Development Team achieve full cross-functionality through self-organization.

- Makes arrangements for scrum events.

- Helps the team members understand aspects of the environment of the organization that they have not yet learned.

Service to the Product Owner

Scrum Master will use his expertise in performing the following duties:

- Helps Product Owner organize Backlog in a suitable manner to maximize product value.

- Use effective management methods for Product Backlog.

- Practice Agile methods.

- Elucidate the items present in the Backlog to the Development Team.

- Arrange Scrum event as and when required.

- Help everyone to understand product-planning set in an empirical backdrop.

Chapter 8: Scrum Theory

Empiricism is the basis for the Scrum Theory. In Empiricism, the governing is based on experience and only if something is known, will the decision be taken. This leads to knowledge states Empiricism. To get the best possible predictability, as well as to control the risk, Scrum Theory uses the incremental method in an iterative manner.

Process control in every empirical process is based on three fundamental rules. While most of us may be familiar with 'inspect and adapt' rules, the third rule namely 'transparency' may not be something you are familiar with.

Transparency: This states that those responsible for the outcome must be aware of or see the aspects of the situation. This means that the observers must share a common understanding as to what is happening based on some accepted standard of discerning things.

Inspection: The inspection at the point of work helps the team arrive at the best solution. Inspection must be detailed so that a complete understanding of the situation is arrived at by the team. At the same time, too many inspections will tend to confuse the issue.

Adapt: Change to accommodate the difference -- this step follows the inspection stage. If the difference is too huge, then the change may become too tedious.

Scrum Events

Prescribed events help to maximize interactions and minimize the need for meetings. Events themselves are time-boxed. They have a minimum and maximum duration but they cannot be altered once you begin a Sprint. Sprint is the container for all events. Every event is an opportunity to 'inspect and adapt' to something new.

The Sprint

This is the essence of Scrum in that everything transpires according to these Sprints. The normal duration of a Sprint is between 3 -- 4 weeks. Within each Sprint, a useable "Done" product increment is created by the Development Team. When one Sprint concludes the next one begins. Main components of the Sprint are these:

- Sprint Planning

- Daily Scrums

- Development Work

- Sprint Review

- Sprint Retrospective

Care is taken to see that the Sprint Goal remains constant throughout the duration of the Sprint. Quality is sustained as pre-determined. When more information is received, the scope may be renegotiated by the Product Owner with the Development Team. Sprints thus define what is to be built and outline the plan for building it. It may be surmised as a mini-project with a time limit for achieving the target fixed at a one-month maximum. When this limit is exceeded, the product may change too much to be relevant and give rise to complexities in the delivery. Sprints help us ensure adjustment through consistent examination by upholding a Sprint Goal fixed for one month. This confines the risk to a one month cost alone.

Sprint Cancellation

Only the Product Owner, whether influenced by the stakeholders, Scrum Master, and the Team members or not, can cancel a Sprint. When the Sprint Goal loses significance, this action will be precipitated. Such an eventuality might arise due to market vagrancy or sudden changes in the technology field. However, since Sprints are of short duration, the cancellation will not influence the final outcome of the project. Sprint cancellation can be traumatic and therefore needs to be avoided. If such a cancellation does occur, all acceptable "Done" products are Okayed by the Product Owner. The rest are put back on the Product Backlog. The work now needs reevaluation.

Planning the Sprint

All members of the Scrum Team gather to plan the Sprint.

This tells the team what work is expected of them that month. The time-box for a one-month Sprint should be only 8 hours though the time durations could be made shorter. The Scrum Master is responsible for conducting the event. He explains the nature of the duties to each of the team members. General issues that would be considered are this:

- In this Sprint, what work must we deliver in the course of the increment?

- How will we deliver this increment?

- What improvements can be incorporated in this Sprint?

Newest Increments Selected for Work

In the first case, the Development Team will decide what portion of the work needs to be done first. They go over the Product Backlog items and check which comes first on the priority list. They add the items that when taken together will fulfill the Sprint Goal. Contributions from all the members of the team will go into finalizing the Sprint increment that must be delivered. The Product Owner decides on the type and amount of change that is required to the Product Backlog.

The input items would comprise of newest increment needed for the Backlog, the Backlog itself, and the record of past performance by the Development Team and its work capacity. The Development Team decides the volume of work it will undertake by deciding the number of items it should take up.

Fixing the Sprint Goal

Following this selection, the Scrum team decides on the Sprint Goal. Here the aim of work is outlined. The Development Team is briefed on why they need to achieve this target of increment.

Now the entire team gets down to how they are going to achieve this target. The product Backlog items are reviewed and the Development Team decides on how to convert it into a "Done" product increment. The Product Backlog now becomes the items chosen from the Backlog along with the plan to convert them into an increment.

Trade-offs before Beginning

The Development Team now sets about coordinating the work with the system used for conversion. The entire work is broken down into small units that take one day to complete. Here, the team members execute trade-offs with the Product Owner.

If some developers feel that the work is too much to be completed in one day (or too little), they will bring it up with the Product Owner. If there is a need for technical intervention (or domain service advice), the team members will ask for suitable outside help.

Sprint Planning thus concludes when the Development Team has arrived at a satisfactory explanation on how they will deliver the increment within the conclusion of the Sprint through the process of self-organizing. The Scrum Master and Product Owner will decide if this is enough before concluding the Sprint Planning session.

Sprint Goal: We see this as the sum of the functionality that contributes to the common objective of delivering the increment "Done" product. Different units within the team have different starting points. They must work to achieve their target within the fixed time-scale. So, when work proceeds within the Development Team, everyone works to achieve a target.

Look from a New Perspective

We can see this as cooking a lunch for 50 people. One set of people works to make the salad. One set works to prepare the meat. Another set of workers is busy with the dough for the bread. They begin at the same time. When they finish, they all arrive at that point in time when the lunch is ready to be eaten.

Or we can see this as the work in a garment factory where tailors are working in conjunction with each other. The material to be stitched is handed out to the tailors. Here the material is the Product Backlog. The tailors represent the Development Team. Their supervisor is the Scrum Master. One portion of the tailors works on fashioning the arms of the garment. Another set of tailors works on the pockets. Yet another set will be working on making the fronts and backs of the garment. They begin together (at the commencement of the Sprint) and finish making the garment (to achieve the Sprint Goal).

"Done" Product

The skill set in each work (project) is different. The concept for both remains the same -- delivering the increment "done" product. Where it differs from software development or management techniques is in the way the "done" product is not 'consumed' at once. It keeps undergoing refinement until the product is perfect for the consumer. This stage will be determined by the Product Owner who will keep altering the Backlog to improve the functionality of the final product

Chapter 9: Daily Scrum

This is a routine event that analyses the work done the previous day and determines what should be done on the present day. To simplify matters, this action (meeting between the Scrum members) needs to be organized at the same place always. This will avoid needless confusion. During this meeting, each member of the Development Team will explain how they contributed to the objective of meeting the Sprint Goal. Then, they explain what they intend to do on the present day and point out any impediments that they are likely to face (or are facing).

Each impediment is analyzed based on how the work is proceeding and how far the team is from achieving the Sprint Goal. The members re-plan and adapt to self-organize the entire team into one cohesive working unit. The Scrum Master enforces the rule that only the members of the Development Team be present at the Daily Scrum. This meeting will be time-boxed for a maximum of 15 minutes. This inspect-and-adapt meeting helps speed up communication, remove bottlenecks, helps spread knowledge of the work progress, and does away with other unnecessary meetings.

Sprint Review

At this stage of the Scrum Framework, a meeting takes place between the stakeholders and the Scrum Team. Achievement of the latest Sprint is balanced against the Product Backlog. This 4-hour time-boxed status meeting is brought to order by the Scrum Master. Key points of this Sprint Review are as follows:

- Development Team, Scrum Master, Product Owner and the stakeholders invited by the Product Owner attend the meeting mandatorily.

- The Product Owner ticks off all the items in the product Backlog as "Done or Not done."

- The Development Team explains the existing working conditions - the advantages and shortfalls, along with problems and solutions.

- They also explain anything about the "Done" increment that the Sprint Review attendees need to know.

- This meeting paves the way for the Sprint Planning. Everyone discusses the status of the product and give suggestions for achieving the best result.

- An overview of the product in the context of its present market value is presented and discussed.

- The review is done on budget and timeline, as also market release and possibilities that could ensue.

The new Product Backlog that arises out of the Sprint Review has been adjusted for new market conditions. It also features new items that everyone feels must be added. This new Backlog will be taken up for the next Sprint.

Sprint Retrospective

This three-hour time-boxed meeting is arranged right after the Sprint Review and before Sprint Planning takes place for the next Sprint. Here every improvement that needs to be included will be discussed. For Sprints shorter than one month, the Sprint Retrospective will be shorter. In this meeting, the things that come into focus are these:

- How was the conduct of the last Sprint? Did the process, tools, relationship and people have a congenial time?

- Keep track of all things that went off successfully -- make sure the improvements needed are marked out.

- Suggest improvements for the Scrum Team to incorporate.

The Scrum Master is always looking for ways to make improvements to the Scrum Team. For this purpose, the "Done" product is assumed to be adequate. This is the formal adaptation time for the Scrum Team to implement changes.

Scrum Artifacts

Scrum artifacts serve the purpose of making things easy for everybody. Thus, everyone is able to inspect and adapt using an artifact. These are values or work that remain transparent. The Product Backlog is one such artifact.

Product Backlog: This is never complete until the final delivery of the product has taken place. The Product Owner maintains it at all times. Every Sprint will result in additions or modifications to the Product Backlog. It reflects the overall progress at any given point in the Scrum Framework. The availability, the contents and the maintenance is solely governed by the Product Owner.

By studying the Product Backlog, one can understand the features, the enhancements, requirements and functions of the product. Changes in the value of this living artifact happen due to market fluctuations or change in technology related to the product.

When multiple Scrum Teams work on the same product, a Product Backlog Attributes will help to group items pertaining to each group. For one group may be working on the functioning aspect, while another group will be working out the marketing strategy. Each team will need the product to have some essential features and this must be included in the Product backlog.

Product refinement helps add fine detail to items in the Product Backlog. The Product Owner does this either alone or in collaboration with the Scrum Master and the Development Team. Higher ordered items have more details than lower ordered items. This type of refinement helps the

Development Team bring one item to "Ready" state before the end of the Sprint.

Sprint Backlog: This forms another artifact that integrates the progress of the product towards the Goal. In reality, it is the plan that has been formulated taken together with the Product Backlog items that will be delivered as increments for achieving the Sprint Goal. New work is added on a daily basis from the Daily Scrum so that the emerging Sprint Backlog will reflect the work to be done and that completed on a daily basis. This highly visible real-time projection of work under progress helps improve quality of feedback and realize increments that have value added at every stage. This is handled entirely by the Development Team.

Increment: All the Sprint Backlog items that are included in achieving the goal go towards making the increment. At the end of each Sprint, the increment is presented in a "Done" form meaning it can be used. This does not mean that it will actually be used.

Artifact Transparency

Transparency of artifacts augments the value of the product and ratifies the rightness of the decisions. The possibility of flaw is diminished greatly. This is the reason Scrum relies so heavily on Artifact Transparency.

Complete transparency is achievable through diligent effort on the part of the Scrum Master, the Product Owner, and stakeholders. The Development Team works to create items that improve transparency based on the instructions given by the Scrum Master. This is important for avoiding hurdles that could crop up any time.

The Scrum Master has the ability to detect incomplete transparency and take corrective action. When the actual result varies from the expected result, he studies the working of the team and suggests corrections. He does not tell them what to do but rather asks for another form of deployment in the action. He directs the Scrum Team to learn and change. They, in turn, work with the organization to bring about the Scrum methodology into place.

Definition of Done

To arrive at the full definition of "Done", this state of affairs must be an acceptable form for everyone. When there is adequate transparency, the work completed will be satisfying to all the people involved. This shared understanding of work completed is defined as "Done".

When the Development Team compiles its list of Product Backlog items, it uses the definition of "Done" to understand how to proceed and how much can be done in that Sprint. This definition sets the minimum work limit for the Scrum Team.

Other agile methods

A few more methods for software development in Agile comprise of Agile Unified Process, Crystal Clear Methods Kanban (Development), Feature Driven Development (FDD), Information Technology Infrastructure Library (ITIL), Joint Application Development (JAD), Lean Development (LD), PRINCE2, Rapid Application Development (RAD) Spiral, Systems Development Life Cycle (SDLC), (Traditional) and Rational Unified Process (RUP) and Extreme Programming.

These implement different lifecycles and so vary from each other. Agile development is required in areas like coding, modeling, process, project management and design. Among them, the most noteworthy ones are Domain-driven Design (DDD), Planning poker, Continuous integration, Pair programming, Story-driven modeling, and User Story. Here is a brief look at some of the aspects of a few methods.

Domain-driven Design

This technique in software development links implementation with the model that is evolving. It is based on a technique of making complex designs on a model domain, basing the primary focus on the domain logic and core domain and employing domain experts with technical capabilities to refine the conceptual model until all problems are solved.

Pair Programming

In this technique, two programmers work simultaneously at one workstation. One becomes the driver - writes code - while the other assumes the role of the navigator -- who watches the code as it is written. Every other day (or hour) they switch roles.

Story-driven Modeling

This software development technique is object-oriented modeling. They use class diagrams and example scenarios to evolve the program structure.

Lean Software Development

Developed by Mary and Tom Poppendieck, this method presents 22 tool set and makes a comparison to the Agile method of management. The principles of this method tell us to eliminate waste, amplify learning, empower the team, deliver as fast as possible, decide as late as possible, see the whole, and build integrity.

Kanban Development

This method is used for managing knowledge networks. In the context of software development, it is a combination of Lean method and a visual-process combination. The system regulates the product and the quantity.

Crystal Clear

This software development methodology is one of the Agile techniques for software management. It is people based and becomes operable if you use certain methods like the Reflective improvement, repeated conveyance of code to users and osmotic communication. It emphasizes factors like personal safety, easy access, and focus.

Chapter 10: Information Technology Infrastructure Library (ITIL)

Aligning the Needs of the Common IT User

With the increase in the multiplicity of applications and technologies, we see a spiraling growth of user-oriented languages and methodologies. There is no concurrency in the way the people use the technology. In order to provide a unified approach for using Information Technology, the Information Technology Infrastructure Library (ITIL) was formed.

The basic core of this literature is based on five volumes that map all that one needs. The Service Lifecycle as defined by ITIL takes you through the primary customer needs identification first. It then details the drivers of IT requirements. Then we step through the design section and learn the details of how the service is implemented. In the final phase, one learns about monitoring aspects and how one may improve the service. The five volumes of ITIL are:

- Service Strategy

- Service Design

- Service Transition

- Service Operation

- Service Continual Service Improvement

Understanding ITSM and its Orientation to ITIL

For businesses, the need to have an effective IT management system takes preference over everything else. IT Service Management (ITSM) comprise of functions and services that lead to a particular solution. Essentially, the ITSM must have these components:

- Service Desk

- Network

- Database

- Project Management

- Incident Management

- Change Management

The simplest form of a business network would be a pizza center intent on expanding their business and governing it by use of IT methods. The more efficient your Service Desk is, the more satisfied the customers will be. This is a single-point-of-contact for everyone in the network. Employees working at the pizza center interact with the customers and their one focus will be this Service Desk. Keeping your Service Desk well -oiled will help you speed up interactions and satisfying customers.

Simplest definition of a network is the combination of two or more computers linked together. It has the potential to deliver solutions suitable for commercial and domestic applications.

Any network needs information about the customers or involved people like age, address, their interests, and their status. This is all compiled in the Database. It is organized to provide up-to-date information that is required for the business or the social network to function smoothly.

Once a definite course of action has been agreed upon, the blueprint is drawn up to improve the functionality of a concern. This is Change Management that includes processes vital to the functioning and improvement of the process. All changes are assessed by the system and the appropriate decision will be enforced to keep the system working at peak efficiency.

In the Incident Management, hazards are analyzed and the conditions leading to the occurrence of the incident are studied. The steps to avert the future occurrence of the incident are incorporated into the system. Further, the system is corrected to adapt to correct the hazard if it occurs again.

In summary, we have Project Management, which comprises of all skills, interpretation and use of approaches and systems that lead to the desired goal. As per the definition presented in the ITIL published volumes, service presented to the client must have value but must not incur costs, must be a single, intelligible object that the customer considers tangible and manageable.

This continuous study takes place in the fields of Governance Methods and Scalability. Through the use of various Study Aids, Case Studies are conducted to see the circumstances that lead to Quick Wins. Other than this, the definition of Qualification and the use of Templates prove useful. Let us look at these topics and check what are Executive Skills and Specialty Topics and how to use knowledge and Skills to the pertinent fields.

Advantages Of Using Itil

Through the use of this technique we stand to gain in the following manner:

1. Enhanced Judgment Creation

2. Improved Client Gratification

3. Perfect Organizational Structure

4. Clear-cut Monetary Supervision

5. Developed Facility Convenience

A Better Look at ITIL Roles and Its Impact

In order to develop a clearer perspective of the internal mechanism within the ITIL framework (as per the ITIL V3 definition), one needs to understand the different roles that there are. Here we can study why each role is different and necessary for the overall perfection of the system. A clear understanding of the various ITIL roles helps to finalize responsibilities within the framework.

Service Strategy

Like in all commercial ventures, Service Strategy revolves around developing a positive rapport with customers. To achieve this end, an effective means to satisfy them must evolve. Hence, Service Strategy lifecycle will determine what services are optimally suited for the customer. Alongside this, the capabilities needed for the conduct of the lifecycle will also be estimated. The market situation and competition will be evaluated on a comparative basis to assess the market status.

Service Portfolio Manager

In this role, the Service Portfolio Manager will handle the menu list of the service provider. He will detail and elaborate on the offerings that customers can avail of if desired. He highlights the capabilities of the service provider. In doing so, he develops and decides on the optimum strategy that is in line with the policy of the IT Steering Group (ISG). The customer gets a feel and looks at the services through the Service Portfolio Manager.

Service Strategy Manager

Another new role introduced in ITIL 2011, the Service Strategy Manager helps implement the service strategy. He maintains communications and builds support for the ISG. His help in producing the service strategy for the service provider in absolutely vital. He further maintains this in his capacity.

Demand Manager

This is also a new role introduced in ITIL 2011 for the taking care of the Demand Management techniques. One of the basic things that the Demand Manager does is to identify the volumetric need of the customer. Then, he verifies that the service provider has the capability to provide the needed output. He further anticipates customer demand for services. His responsibility lies in understanding customer need and influencing the customer demand.

IT Steering Group

Senior members of the management in the business and the top echelon of the IT department take part in the IT Steering Group. Their responsibilities include devising the strategy and helping finalize the direction of the IT services that they provide to the customer. Various development projects and programs are prioritized according to the urgency and needs of the customer. The IT Steering Group aligns the business in the direction of the IT strategy that is being adopted at any particular time.

Financial Manager

The Financial Manager in the ITIL framework will handle all finance related activities. He prepares the budget for the IT service provider. He takes care of the accounting too. The preparation of the bill and handling of accounts in this regard will be also within the purview of the Financial Manager.

Business Relationship Manager

This role is comparatively new and was introduced only in 2011. The roles of the Business Relationship Manager and the Service Level Manager have several overlapping regions. The Business Relationship Manager primarily works to identify the customer and the customer needs. It is his or her responsibility to keep the relationship on a positive basis identifying ups and downs of the list of demands the customer makes. He interacts with the service provider to ensure the needs are met. He further runs through the service catalog to see that the entire range of demands is covered.

Chapter 11: Service Design

This segment of the framework looks after the IT Service design. It provides new designs, makes amends to previous designs to suit new parameters and helps improve quality. These roles mentioned below are imperative to the proper functioning of the ITIL service framework.

Service Owner

In many instances, the Service Owner will be at the head of a team of technical experts and groups of allied support teams. He undertakes to provide certain services agreed on a bilateral basis with the customer. He is involved in the execution of Operational Level Agreements. His counterpart in the ITIL framework is the Service Level Manager. In essence, he owns (or hires) the infrastructure that is required to provide the service to the customer.

Service Catalog Manager

The various services the Service Owner provides are mentioned in the catalog. This is kept current by the Service

Catalog Manager through consultations with the Service Owner and the various groups within the framework. This helps the customer make an informed choice when seeking services.

Information Security Manager

The Information Security Manager holds a huge responsibility. He will give assurance for the privacy, reliability, and accessibility of assets and data within the organization. These will include IT services and information. His work will be interlinked with Security Management network to a greater extent than with the actual IT work done by the company. Other than phone calls and interdepartmental communications, the work of the Information Security Manager will involve paperwork and building links.

Capacity Manager

Determining the short or long term goals of the organization with an eye on the available resources is the main duty of the Capacity Manager. He will ensure service and infrastructural capability is adequate to handle the customer requirement. The performance target will always be within his purview so that the company is able to meet the capacity that they agreed to deliver.

Technical Analyst

The technical aspects that are vital for designing and operating IT services will come under the wings of the Technical Analyst. The IT structure infrastructure management will be supported by the technical expertise of the Technical Analyst. This role that involves technical management is important for improving IT services through testing. You will find one or more technical analysts in every core sector of the company. Further, he will have the capabilities to help develop the skills needed within the IT infrastructure.

Service Level Manager

The Service Level Manager prepares reports by monitoring all service levels. He ensures Service Level Agreements are adhered to at all times. He oversees the Underpinning Contracts and Operational Level Agreements. He further ensures that the Management Processes are appropriate. This way he will help the service provider meet the set service level target.

Risk Manager

In the ITIL framework, the Risk Manager will help in identifying the risks present and probable within the organizational structure. He will devise the strategy to help mitigate the risk. Control of risks will be ensured through proper estimation and evaluation. All assets are listed and assessed for risks and threats. The vulnerability of each asset is cataloged and risk management measures are enforced.

Enterprise Architect

Essential architectural components of the business are maintained in the Enterprise Architecture. The Enterprise Architect will ensure that all the listings are accurate and benefit the organization. When the organization is huge, there may be several roles under this category. The Infrastructure Architect may handle the immovable assets. The Business Architect will help with the listing of the business assets. The Information Architect and the Application Architect will handle the information and applications categories respectively.

Availability Manager

The Availability Manager has a dual role in the framework. One is to ensure availability of the IT services through analysis and observation. The other is to ensure that the processes and tools are appropriate for meeting the agreed service level target. He defines, analyzes and plans the various aspects of the IT service. Through measurement, he lays in place the needed improvements. He oversees the roles and infrastructure to ensure compatibility with the work in hand.

Supplier Manager

Governing the operations related the suppliers and supplier obligations rest with the Supplier Manager. This ensures that work is worth the money paid to the suppliers. He clarifies the needs of the organization to the suppliers and ensures that these are met adequately. He looks over the contractual agreements to keep all suppliers in line.

Service Design Manager

All the design documents are prepared and maintained by the Service Design Manager. He ensures that all designs meet safety standards and have adequate quality. He will be involved in all improvements to standards and services provided to the customer.

IT Service Continuity Manager

This role is for managing some of the serious risks that could disrupt the working of the organization. IT Service Continuity Manager will make sure that a minimum agreed level of work will always be in progress at all times. This often is the situation in the aftermath of an accident or mishap. He then takes steps to rectify the damage and bring the services back to even keel.

Compliance Manager

For the organization, the Compliance Manager ensures the uniformity in approach. Consistent accounting practices make sure that the organization meets the legal requirements as a responsible concern. He makes sure that standards for use of tools and appliances are adhered to. He enforces proper guidelines for work practices that are within safety and quality standards.

Applications Analyst

A single or a group of Applications Analysts is needed for ensuring the smooth progress of processes and integrity of functions used. He will help the team members develop skills required to operate within the framework and output the IT product that the customer wants. This person is important for testing and deploying application-oriented aspects within the lifecycle. In this Applications Management role, the applications are maintained through the length of their lifecycle. Improvements are possible by testing the IT services at various levels.

Service Transition

Project Manager

The Project Manager will be responsible for the Release of the product that the customer desires. He makes a study of all resources that are available. He works out the necessary skill set and the amount of work that should be undertaken to deliver the product. Further, he draws up the plan to work out the schedule to meet the time and volume targets for the Release. Everybody in the framework is answerable to him.

Application Developer

The IT Services requires certain applications and working systems to achieve full functionality. This entire work comes under the purview of the Application Developer. He will customize products supplied by the Software Vendors. In addition to this, he will develop and maintain certain custom applications.

Configuration Manager

To deliver the IT services, certain Configuration items are required. The Configuration Manager maintains the information for this. For doing this, he or she will maintain a logical model. This model will contain the IT infrastructure components along with their associations.

Release Manager

The Release Manager arranges for a Release considering time and cost estimates. He maintains quality and coordinates resources. His plan will be useful for the overall strategy.

Change Advisory Board (CAB)

The Change Manager will handle all the changes within the framework. He gets the assessment and recommendations from the Change Advisory Board (CAB). This group tells the scheduling and priorities to the Change Manager.

Emergency Change Advisory Board (ECAB)

High impact emergency changes might make it necessary for deploying a smaller sub-group known as the Emergency Change Advisory Board (ECAB). This group is constituted from the members of the CAB. Membership is decided by coming together at a meeting of the CAB when there is an emergency situation.

Test Manager

The responsibilities of the Test Manager will include ensuring that the IT services will have the capability to handle the new Releases. In addition, he ensures that this will be in alignment with the needs of the customer.

Change Manager

In the lifecycle of changes, the decision to modify the

volumes or set time limits will be with the Change Manager. He starts and stops the lifecycle. He ensures that the IT services carry on without any interruptions. He makes sure that the changes incorporated will be useful to the company and the customer. If there are circumstances where the changes are out of the ordinary, he will consult the CAB for further instructions on how and when he should make changes.

Knowledge Manager

The first task of the Knowledge Manager is to ensure that there is no repetition in the cycle of discovering knowledge. Further, he will see to it that the IT firm is able to gather and store knowledge in an efficient manner. He also takes part in the analyzing and sharing of knowledge as the situation warrants.

Chapter 12: Service Operation

1ST Level Support

Incidents received by this First Level Support group may be standard requests for service or it may be an incident of failure of IT service at some point in the lifecycle framework. The group registers and classifies the incident. All attempts are made to rectify the problem as soon as possible. When an immediate solution is not presentable, the incident is passed on to the Second Level Support group. The expert support group will handle the incident from that point onwards. In case the request is for Service, the group will take up the work. The progress will be conveyed on an ongoing basis to the requester.

2nd Level Support

This group will handle all incidents that cannot be solved by the First Level Support. The Second Level Support might rope in outside help say in the software consultation or hardware installation from qualified people in that field. Like before, the aim is to restore the service as soon as possible so that the loss is minimized. There are times when a solution will not be found. Then, they will pass the incident on to Problem Management.

3rd Level Support

This group handles incidents that the Second Level Support find impossible to solve. In normal cases, the problems will be in the software or the hardware portion of the IT services manufacturers and suppliers. Once they receive a request from the Second Level Support, they will move as quickly as possible to find the proper solution.

Problem Manager

The Problem Manager handles all Problems and Problem lifecycles. He makes a study of the incidence of Problems and the time that the incident occurs. The impact of the incident on the outcome of IT product is also documented. Then, the Problem Manager will take steps to see that the impact is reduced and the likelihood of such an incident occurring is circumvented.

Incident Manager

The Incident Manager carries out the implementation of all processes in Incident Management. When incidents cannot be resolved within the Service Levels, the company will turn to the Incident Manager to find a solution. He thereby will be responsible for preventing the escalation of incidents.

Access Manager

When regular users want access to a service, the Access Manager will help them out. He takes steps to assure that unauthorized users do not access the service. In keeping with the policy defined under the Information Security Management, he will carry out essential tasks to streamline overall functioning.

Major Incident Team

This group will work under the Incident Manager. They consist of technical specialists and IT management staff. They will be called up when there is a Major Incident. They work together to resolve the problem in the shortest possible time.

Facilities Manager

All the corporeal surroundings that house the IT company infrastructure are administered by the Facilities Manager. This will include the power and lighting for the buildings, the ventilation and cooling systems and access to the buildings. He will also be responsible for all the environmental issues coming from the physical aspects of the company.

Service Request Fulfilment Group

The First Level Service group handles common requests. When the issues are complicated the Service Request Fulfilment Group is summoned. They handle all the special requests arising in the company.

IT Operator

The IT Operators are company staff involved in routine activities. They will carry out scheduled tasks and perform backups where and when needed. Standard equipment will be used to service the customer.

IT Operations Manager

The IT Operations Manager handles Service Operational Activities. Other than this overall responsibility, he will also ensure the timely conduct of all activities. This will increase the operational efficiency of everyone concerned.

Continual Service Improvement

Process Owner

This role is essential for ensuring that the process selected will be suitable for the achieving the ends of the customer. The Process Owner will be responsible for continuously monitoring the process and ensuring the correct metrics are observed. His other responsibilities include managing sponsorship, monitoring improvements and managing the overall functioning. When the infrastructure is huge, the Process Owner will be separate from the Process Manager. Process Manager will take the responsibility for operational management.

Process Architect

The Process Architecture is essential for the seamless operation of all processes. The Process Architect manages this. Usually a part of the Enterprise Architecture, the

Process Architecture also includes the Process Owners. All changes to the processes are done by the Process Architect.

CSI Manager

The responsibility of the Continuous Service Improvement (CSI) Manager is to deploy improvements that help the process achieve a better manifestation and efficiency. Other than the work, the cost aspect will also be monitored for more effectiveness. The CSI Manager will oversee processes within the infrastructure that can be improved, including those provided by the service providers. This he will bring into effect by measuring the various parameters.

Outside Roles In It Organization

Customer

The person who buys the IT service is the customer. The Service Provider will chalk out strategies and agree on Service Levels that will help maintain the quality of the output. Work will begin once the agreement has been drawn up.

Service User

The Service User is a person who uses the services directly on a continuous basis. In this respect, he differs from the Customer who is only interested in the end product. The Service User may use service from several IT service providers at the same time.

Improvement of ITIL V3 over the Previous Version ITIL V2

We see an addition in the number of processes alongside functions in the newer version of ITIL. While ITIL V2 had only 2 functions and 10 functions the ITIL V3 has additional 2 functions (4 in all) and 26 processes. The focus and approach also have been refined. The focus previously was on service design and service strategy alone in the new version we see an overall equal attention to all processes. The approach has also shifted from the being process oriented to one that is based on the lifecycle.

In the security department, the older version had security integrated as a part of the evaluation while the new version the security management has become a process that is separate. In both, ITIL focuses on product, people, and process but in ITIL V3, there is an additional focus on the partner.

Details of the Service Lifecycle Process and Function

The service lifecycle forms the framework for ITIL. To enhance the effectiveness of service management, in each lifecycle, a certain procedure will be demarcated. Service Strategy is continuously involved in the Measurement and Evaluation while Continual Service Improvement keeps track of development and makes changes that will help improve the system further.

At the core, again depending on the requirements Service Design, Service Transition and Service Operations will be taking place. Service lifecycle helps improve service management approach through a better comprehension of the structure. Each lifecycle will interact with a certain process and function in a particular manner.

The tools or the personnel required to perform a function, process or activity is termed as the function, while the actual work instructions will define the process. As mentioned previously, we have 26 processes and 4 functions.

Overview of Service Strategy

Service Strategy defines the basic aspects required to comprehend and outperform the competition on a continuing basis.

KEY BENEFITS OF USING ITIL

ITIL Service Management framework is immensely useful for the professional and organizations. A look at the significant competences shows these points:

- Be able to handle various possibility including risks resulting from diverse business requirements

- Provide sustenance for all types of business results

- Enhance customer involvement

- Empower modification in trade dealings

- Demonstrate worth for money input

- Constantly develop with small changes

This increased functionality provides a wider scope for deploying various parameters and realizing a better outcome. These are the ways to get a better edge using ITIL Management.

Advantages within the Framework for ITIL Users

- Show through actual values and volumes that your service is valuable

- Make sure that the service providers you employ are giving your value for your money

- Keep the customer expectations in view at all times so that your service never falls short in quality

- Ensure that you have a low-risk working atmosphere that is conducive to change and responsive to customer needs

- Help you circumvent service disruptions and thereby help your customer too.

- Take care of the risks that your business will have

- Allow better customer interaction to build positive rapport that will make business improve significantly

- Make the access to your services such that your customers are always able to use them anywhere and at any time

- Keep a strict tab on service levels so that you are able to read the returns accurately

- Keep service disruptions to the minimum

- Help marketing aspect for your services so that consumption of your goods is more

- Get accurate projection to respond most appropriately to demand in an encouraging way so that costs are lowered

Chapter 13: ITIL Checklists - Use of Templates

ITIL document templates serve as ITIL Process Output checklists. During process execution, they will help as guidelines. The ITIL-2011-compliant Reference Process Model has 102 checklists.

These checklists were designed by APM Group and are licensed ITIL® officially. For first time designers of documents that are ISO 20000 compliant, these will prove useful.

I) ITIL SERVICE STRATEGY TEMPLATE

Financial Analysis

One can cultivate a perception of the cost-effectiveness of the services as it provides all details of the prices. Customers can get a look and compare different items and make an assessment based on the other factors like time of completion in addition to the cost. The Financial Analysis gives an overall picture of the viability and completeness of the project. All the following items of information will be present in this:

Analysis of the service

This is needed to create increments of delivery of the product. One develops an insight into the things required on an immediate time scale. The various aspects that make up the service analysis are given below.

1. Service value potential

2. Contending options

3. Relative benefits

4. Costs involved
    4.1. Costs per service according to type
        4.1.1. Direct costs
        4.1.2. Indirect costs

5. Profitability
    5.1. Each service profit margin
    5.2. Actual revenues got from each service

6. Trends
    6.1. Listing of unviable options in services
    6.2. Services that do not have much market value
    6.3. Services with declining demand
    6.4. Services that will incur loss

7. Variable dynamics in pricing
   7.1. Service demand thresholds that make the service provider to invest significant amounts
   7.2. Changes in cost estimates based on increasing or decreasing service demand
   7.3. Actual to the Planned Spending

8. Itemize for all items in the Financial budget:
   8.1. Prediction
   8.2. Actual spending amount

9. Variation analysis
   9.1. Customer probability
      9.1.1. Profit expectable from each customer
      9.1.2. Revenue got from each customer

10. Options for Funds
    10.1. Outsourcing
    10.2.   Leasing
    10.3.   Owning

11. Asset valuation
    11.1. Value of infrastructural components
    11.2. Value estimates of assets that are intangible

12. Post-program Analysis
    12.1. In the case of project investment
       12.1.1.   Business case
    12.2. In terms of budget spent
    12.3. Realization of actual benefits
    12.4. Realized benefits

SERVICE PORTFOLIO

This portfolio lists all the services that the service provider is giving to the customer. Some services that are directly related to the business will be seen openly by the customer (SLA). While others that involve the infrastructure portion of the service will remain hidden (maybe UC). You will find three main categories in the Service Portfolio.

1. Service Pipeline

2. Service Catalog

3. Retired Service

The service will be branched from the common business activity they are closely linked to. The customer will not be able to see all the services. This portfolio will remain as a part of the CMS. One must endeavor to maintain this as a dedicated database. You can also maintain it in a series of linked documents having a hierarchical structure.

In each service, the Service Portfolio will comprise of the following items:

1. Name of the service

2. Status at this point of time: Designed, Proposed, Released, Chartered, Retired, Tested, Defined, Operational, Built

3. Type of the service: Visible -- that delivered to the customer or Invisible -- that which is not seen by the customer and used for underpinning the value delivered to the customers

4. Service Owner

5. Customers

6. Procedure for signing up (Contacts and methods of approach): i) Contact details of Service Level Manager and ii) Signing up procedure

7. Outcome that customer seeks (target):
   7.1. Business outcome that supports the customer
   7.2. Guaranteed outcome as in terms of quality

8. Justification from value point of view

9. Increase in utility

10. Packages and choices
    10.1. Packages of different Service Levels that the customer can choose from
    10.2. Packages for different time or geographical zones
    10.3. Packages with increased utility
    10.4. Price of packages and services

11. Standard pricing scheme

12. Penalties and deductions for different schemes

13. Other Dependencies

14. Configuration items like hardware, software, staff, document and sub-types like printer, server.

15. Services

15.1. Infrastructural services that will help deliver this service (documentation needed for planning)

15.2. Supported services -- those that depend on this service (policy -- all things will depend on this)

16. Changes that are on the anvil
    16.1. Priority allocated to the proposed change
    16.2. Time schedule along with present status

17. Cost-benefit analysis (Business case)
    17.1. List of associated risks
    17.2. Plan reference namely -- entry in CSI Register, Strategic Action Plan.

II) ITIL SERVICE DESIGN TEMPLATE

The checklist SLA - OLA in the Service Design category shows the agreement drawn up by the service provider. The SLA or the Service Level Agreement is to the customer while the OLA is with another group operating within the same company for the delivery of some infrastructural service.

The SLA will detail out the viewpoint of the service to be provided from the point of view of the customer. The Service Catalog definition will form the basis for the template. It will show responsibilities shared or otherwise and specify the work targets. In the process of the Service Design, the SLA becomes a form of the Service Level Requirements. In order to avoid duplication and ease the work approach, a multi-tiered structure is adopted for the SLA. Usually, this is of three layers.

1. Customer level

2. Corporate level

3. Service level

At the customer level, a customer or a group of customers will be the target group. The scope will end when the demarcation goes out of the group. At the Corporate level, the emphasis is on all the customers and the business interaction that helps the organization maintains its high market profile and functionality. The Service level is self-explanatory. The focus will be on all the services that the company wants to provide to the customer.

CONTENTS OF SLA

The common SLA will have these items in it:

1. Service name

2. Desired outcome as per the customer

3. Customer side business processes that is available on the agenda of service provider

4. Warranty in specified segments

5. Special utility that the customer can avail of in certain conditions

6. Justification of the business benefits

7. Criticality of assets and the services

7.1. Estimates provided for disruption to service or loss of assets through a categorization giving the levels of impact on the business

7.2. Listing out those assets that are critical for the service

7.3. Vital Business Functions (VBFs) present in the framework

7.4. Certain other business data that are critical for the functioning

8. Support levels and types asked for
   8.1. Onsite support
      8.1.1. Specification of areas
      8.1.2. Identifying the types of users
      8.1.3. Resolution times depending on priorities -- defining priorities and reactions to incidents, classification of incidents
      8.1.4. Types of infrastructure that is supported by the service
   8.2. Support through remote communication
      8.2.1. Specification of areas
      8.2.2. Identifying the types of users
      8.2.3. Resolution times depending on priorities -- defining priorities and reactions to incidents, classification of incidents
      8.2.4. Types of infrastructure that is supported by the service

9. Technical level

10. Description of technological service solution system

11. Model Price
   11.1. Cost for providing service
   11.2. Penalties, rules, and defaults

12. References and links list
    12.1. This list will specify whom to contact in the course of resolution of the solution. It may be to a higher Service level
    12.2. Customer level to which the solution applies
    12.3. Clearance data (place, date)
        12.3.1. At the point of contact of the customer representative
        12.3.2. At the Service Level Manager point of contact

13. Length of duration of contract
    13.1. Dates for the start
    13.2. Dates for the end
    13.3. Rules pertaining to renewal
    13.4. Rules pertaining to termination
    13.5. For special cases, early termination rules will apply

14. Service provider - customer communication
    14.1. Service Reporting: Time period for the service reports and contents to be provided by the service provider
    14.2. Service Reviews: Details of the procedure that performs regular reviews of the service for the customer

15. Complaint handling and exception handling procedures: This will include escalation procedures, response times agreed on a mutual basis, details that are needed for making formal complaints
    15.1. Contact person who will take care of the complaint on the customer side and the contact details

15.2. Satisfaction surveys: Details of the procedure used regularly to measure satisfaction of customer

15.3. Business Relationship Manager assigned to handle queries from the side of the service provider and the procedure of contacting him or her

16. Service times
    16.1. Working times for the service
    16.2. Holidays, exceptions

17. Service level targets
    17.1. Capacity commitments
    17.2. Application response times

18. Specific methodology of reporting performance and capacity

19. Conditions needed to apply scalability assuming there will be an increase in the utilization of service and workload over time

20. Service capacity
    20.1. Enumeration of users and their groups
    20.2. Enumeration of types of transactions
    20.3. Daily, weekly and seasonal variation of business cycle

21. Commitments and targets availability
    21.1. Definitions for Major Incidents: This includes Releases and Emergency situations where it is needed to resolve urgent issues, details of the process for announcing interruptions to planned service

21.2.Availability targets: Keeping in mind the agreed downtime and service time, the definitions are laid down for availability levels

21.3.Maintenance downtime: Pre Notifications for downtime period and number of downtimes allowed or scheduled

22. Procedure for reporting availability

22.1.Reliability targets: Some customers will require this and it is reported in two ways. One is Mean Time between Service Incidents. The other is Mean Time between Failures.

22.2. Maintenance restrictions: This will include seasonal restrictions and the allowed window for maintenance. The methodology to declare planned interruptions is also detailed.

22.3. Conditions when service will be unavailable: This will be applicable for the site where it is announced.

22.4. Maintainability targets: Some of the customers will consider this important. It is the Mean Time to Restore Services

22.5. Service Continuity Commitments: This is important when one has to consider interruption to service.

22.5.1. Detail of the time required for achieving the service level after interruption

22.5.2. Time required for normalization of services

23. Responsibilities entailed in the service

23.1.Duties expected from the service user

23.2. Obligation of the service provider

23.3. Procedure for observing IT security norms

23.4. Obligations on the part of the customer

CAPACITY PLAN CHECKLIST

The Capacity Plan will include scenarios to provide service for different volumes of demand. It helps in planning for the available resources at different service levels. The contents of the Capacity Plan checklist will comprise of the following:

- Prediction of performance/service utilization

- Prediction of performance/resource utilization

- Business Framework

- Expansion/Adjustment for Performance and Service Capacity

- Factors that could impact Performance/Service Capacity

Prediction of Performance/Service Utilization

Here you can see all the specific aspects at every service level as per the Capacity Management plan. This will have the three major subdivisions as follows:

1. Suppositions and database: The forecast needs data and guidelines or suppositions for the functioning of the plan. Study will be centered around these indicators:
   1.1. Unprecedented divergence from the average values
   1.2. Tendencies of data performances from historic and current data for performance and service utilization

1.3. Business side statistics predictions to aid service utilization
1.4. Watch on performance and capacity thresholds that are about to be attained

2. Predictions
   2.1. Forecasts for short-term, medium-term and long-term in:
   2.2. Service utilization
   2.3. Performance

3. Expansion capabilities as per demand
   3.1. All measures to handle extra demand for IT services and resources are detailed herewith. These will be of two kinds:
   3.2. Proposals which have no immediate consequence or utilization
   3.3. Proposals of an immediate nature: This will include ongoing initiatives. You will also find those proposals that are engaging in the concrete planning phase.

Prediction of Performance/Service Utilization

Here we see all IT resources and those components used according to the Capacity Management plan. Like the section above, this will also have three major subdivisions.

1. Suppositions and database: The forecast needs data and guidelines or suppositions for the functioning of the plan. Study will be centered around these indicators:
   1.1. Unprecedented divergence from the average values
   1.2. Tendencies of data performances from historic and current data for performance and service utilization

1.3. Business side statistics predictions to aid service utilization

1.4. Watch on performance and capacity thresholds that are about to be attained

2. Predictions

2.1. Forecasts for short-term, medium-term and long-term in:

2.2. Service utilization

2.3. Performance

3. Expansion capabilities according to demand

3.1. All measures to handle extra demand for IT services and resources are detailed herewith. These will be of two kinds:

3.2. Proposals that have no immediate consequence or utilization.

3.3. Proposals of an immediate nature: This will include ongoing initiatives. You will also find those proposals that are engaging in the concrete planning phase.

Business Framework

This will comprise of two major types of content.

1. Recognized Business Enterprises

1.1. Details and methodology of the initiative

1.2. Expectable outcomes on service/resource capacity and performance

1.3. Tangible solutions to deal with extra demand for IT resources and services

1.3.1. For the long and medium term

1.3.2. For the immediate time -- ongoing assessments or proposals that are actively being promoted

2. Recognized Work Volume Predictions
   2.1. Services that have felt the impact
   2.2. Future impact studies on outputs and asset volumes
   2.3. Tangible solutions to deal with extra demand for IT resources and services
      2.3.1. For the long and medium term
      2.3.2. For the present time -- ongoing evaluations that are actively being promoted
      2.3.3. The kind of work volume

Expansion/Adjustment for Performance and Service Capacity

Analysis of ongoing initiatives or those in the pipeline to adjust performance and service capacity is detailed here. Contents will comprise of the following:

- Person who is responsible for the service

- Name of service

- Business case

- Person under whose care the adjustment is being made

- Details of the change or adjustment

- Price and resources involved

- List of activities

- Infrastructure components that will be affected

- Time schedule

- Current status

- Any other alternative plans

Factors that Impact Performance/Service Capacity

The impact is of three types.

1. Effect due to changes in the organization, contract or regulations

2. Effect due to changes to targets at service level or aspects like continuity or availability

3. Effect due to availability of new technologies and methodologies

UNDERPINNING CONTRACT (UC)

The service provider and some third party undertake this type of contract. The supporting service is the type that is needed by the service provider in order to supply some product or service to the customer. For this reason, it is necessary to align the Underpinning Contracts (UC) along the Service Level Agreements that are customer-facing. All the following information will be provided in the UC:

1. Name of Service Provided

2. Duration for which the contract is valid
   2.1. Start date for contract
   2.2. End date for contract
   2.3. Rules for agreement renewal
   2.4. Rules for agreement termination
   2.5. Other rules concerning early renewal or termination of contract

3. Nature of communication and interaction interfaces: The two parties entering into the contract will have the following conditions:
   3.1. Details and contact procedures for both concerned parties
   3.2. Reporting of service: Intervals of the reports and contents will be shown
   3.3. Complaints handling procedure: Response time to handle exceptions or routine complaints, details that will be necessary when filing a complaint, escalation procedure
   3.4. Interface details for all cases -- between service provider and third party or with any relevant party

4. Service Level -- Targets to be achieved
   4.1. Capacity commitments and service level targets
   4.2. Application response times
   4.3. Specific methodology of reporting performance and capacity
   4.4. Conditions needed to apply scalability assuming there will be an increase in the utilization of service and workload over time

5. Service capacity
   5.1. Enumeration of users and their groups
   5.2. Enumeration of types of transactions
   5.3. Daily, weekly and seasonal variation of business cycle
   5.4. Commitments and performance targets availability

6. Definitions for Major Incidents: This includes Releases and Emergency situations where it is needed to resolve urgent issues, details of the process for announcing interruptions to planned service
   6.1. Availability targets: Keeping in mind the agreed downtime and service time, the definitions are laid down for availability levels
   6.2. Maintenance downtime: Pre Notifications for downtime period and number of downtimes allowed or scheduled

7. Procedure for reporting availability
   7.1. Reliability targets: Some customers will require this and it is reported in two ways. One is Mean Time between Service Incidents. The other is Mean Time between Failures.
   7.2. Maintenance restrictions: This will include seasonal restrictions and the allowed window for maintenance. The methodology to declare planned interruptions is also detailed.
   7.3. Conditions when service will be unavailable: This will be applicable for the site where it is announced.
   7.4. Maintainability targets: Some of the customers will consider this important. It is the Mean Time to Restore Services.

8. Service Continuity Commitments: This is important when one has to consider interruption to service as in the case of disasters.
   8.1. Detail of the time required for achieving the service level after interruption
   8.2. Time required for normalization of services

9. Responsibilities:
   9.1. Duties normally did by service user
   9.2. Obligation expected of the service provider
   9.3. Procedure for keeping IT security norms
   9.4. Obligations on the part of the customer

10. Change History

11. Supplier Details
    11.1. Name of Service Supplier
    11.2. Contact person for supplier and details
    11.3. Supplier number and other information
    11.4. Address information

12. Desired Outcome of the Service
    12.1. Activities required for achieving the result
    12.2. Business processes that have to be undertaken to this end
    12.3. Outcome in terms of utility
    12.4. Outcome in terms of warranty

13. Support Level and Types: We have two kinds of support.
    13.1. Onsite support:
    13.2. Location, sites and areas where it is applicable
    13.3. List of infrastructure that will have support
    13.4. User categories
    13.5. Resolutions times

13.6. Reactions that is expected

14. Remote support
    14.1. Location, sites and areas where it is applicable
    14.2. List of infrastructure that will have support
    14.3. User categories
    14.4. Resolutions times
    14.5. Reactions that is expected

15. Specifications: Details of the standards and related technical specifications for the interactions and interface.

16. Price:

17. Cost for providing service

18. Penalties, rules, and defaults

19. Information for Clearance: In this the date and location are always specified.

20. Service Provider Site Supplier Manager

21. Third party who is responsible for clearance

22. Service Times:

23. Normal times: These are the times when the service is freely available.

24. Exceptions: These will be the holidays and downtimes for maintenance

25. Subcontractors: Third parties will engage subcontractors to carry out their contractual obligations.

26. List of employed subcontractors and their part in carrying out the work

27. Reference method for verifying that the work is proceeding as per the contract

28. References and Links: This list will provide the links and contact people higher up in the Service Level that one must contact if their current level fails.

Service Design Package (SDP)

This checklist and the associated templates come under the Design Coordination category. This Service Design Package (SDP) is derived from the Service Level Requirements. Specifications show how to utilize the various aspects of the service technically with an optimized organizational interaction to serve the customer.

Supporting Services will be bundled together to deliver Business Service. In the process of development of service solution, the SDP will be passed to Service Transition from its current position within the Service Design. Information contained within this package will be:

1. Header: This part gives details of the responsible persons within the service framework. This header portion of the SDP is needed at the start of the project.

2. Service name

3. Name of service owner

4. Clearance details: Here you will have the location of the site with the time and date.
   4.1. Service Design Manager Clearance
   4.2. Service management clearance of the SDP: Here they specify that the needed work will be within the scope of the service provider; any preconditions needed to begin operations will be stated to the customer. People related to the service are given below.
      4.2.1. Information Security Manager
      4.2.2.   Capacity Manager
      4.2.3.   Compliance Manager
      4.2.4.   Availability Manager
      4.2.5.   Financial Manager
      4.2.6.   IT Service Continuity Manager

5. Specifications Detailing Requirements Needed within the Service Transition network: This portion of the template is based on Service Level Requirements and outlines details of the conditions that must be met. Once these conditions are met, the new service will be built based on the information provided. The details will specify the duties that are expected to be fulfilled within the infrastructure and its supported applications.
   5.1. Requirements at the Service Level
   5.2. Compliance Standards that is needed
   5.3. Operational abilities required
   5.4. Functionality that must be present

6. Constraints due to the architecture
   6.1. Requirements to be fulfilled if you want to migrate
   6.2. Access rights required
   6.3. Details of necessary interface

7. Necessities of Information Security

8. Operation of Service with emphasis on development ideas:
   8.1. Operations relating to service
   8.2. Operation functionality requirement: The list of activities and related procedures that will ensure the smooth functioning of the service

9. Management of issues and resolving risks methodology
   9.1. Documentation for end-user and general operational procedures
   9.2. Necessary reporting and measuring alongside monitoring process

10. Skills and human resources required for service functioning
    10.1. Regular Service Enhancement
    10.2. Mechanisms and the methodology that help improve service continually
    10.3. Skills and human resources needed to keep improving the service

11. Blueprint of Implementation of Organizational and Technical Aspects: In this section, you learn the requirements needed to be performed while Service Transition is underway. The four main segments will tell you the details of this in detail.
    11.1. Decomposition: This has the following two segments:
    11.2. Infrastructure Internal Structure that supports the service
    11.3. Name of this particular infrastructure service

11.4. Service Providers (Name of the persons responsible as Service Owners)

Operational Level Agreement (OLA) References

1.1. Changes (if needed) to the OLA as per mutual consent

2. Supporting Services supplied by an external provider
   2.1. Name of the particular external service
   2.2. Supplier name
   2.3. Supplier Manager

3. Underpinning Contract (UC) Reference
   3.1. Changes (if needed) to the UC as per mutual consent

4. Transition Master Plan: This will give the outline of the plan that will put the new strategy into place. It will consist of the following:
   4.1. Deployment plan
   4.2. Testing plan
   4.3. Integration with projects related to the service transition
   4.4. Back-up plan in the case the deployment is a failure

5. Migration details

6. Details of technical nature: This set of details will instruct you on how to build and then deploy the service. In addition to operating the service, you also need to test the service.

7. Base applications customization within the service framework (this will show that the system is based on a custom application or say, the SAP system)

8. Tools required for support
   8.1. Production and putting to use of development appliances, machines, devices and contrivances used for deployment
   8.2. Production and putting to use of development appliances, machines, devices and contrivances used for migration
   8.3. Production and putting to use of development appliances, machines, devices and contrivances used for back-out in case the deployment is not successful
   8.4. Production and putting to use of development appliances, machines, devices and contrivances used for testing

9. Modification necessary for infrastructure: This will comprise of the list of changes that are needed to test and deploy the service. This will also contain the details of building and service operation.
   9.1. Purchase and installation of components for the infrastructure
   9.2. Reconfiguration of components in the infrastructure

10. Changes needed for the organization: This will be the kind of changes that must go into effect for the proper functioning of the organization.
    10.1. Additional personnel required for implementing changes
    10.2. Details that are pertinent to the required resources

10.3. Details for acquiring these resources for your organization

10.4. Necessary skills

    10.4.1. Details of the skills

    10.4.2. Method of getting these skills

10.5. Process changes that are required

    10.5.1. Creation, changing or reorienting IT processes (this include Process Owners)

    10.5.2. Details of the changes needed for the IT processes (design criterion)

11. Resources

    11.1. Building the service: This will be the details and amount required to build the service

    11.2. Operate the service: This will be the details and amount required to operate the service

12. Information for Transition Planning: Here you can find the estimates of resources that are needed and the new time frame for implementing the services. After some time of operation, Release Management or Change Management updates this system. Project Management also has a say in this matter. The Preliminary Service Transition will be discussed here.

    12.1. Milestones and Major: In the project phase, we see these demarcations are necessary tools.

    12.2. Required staff: This is an arbitrary value that is determined by the planned expansion or change.

    12.3. Time schedule: This too is determined by the project goal and time constraints.

Chapter 14: III) ITIL Service Transition Template

This checklist will help you to build the service and make sure it is functioning in a proper manner. It will give you the guidelines for regulated implementation of changes. The main topics covered by this template would be:

Change Management:

Control of the lifecycle of changes would be the objective of Change Management. It ensures that beneficial changes are made and that the disruption to the IT services is minimal.

Change Evaluation:

When you need to do major changes to the infrastructure or you deploy a new service, you need to assess the change. This type of assessment will keep the Change lifecycle in synchrony with the goal of the service process.

Project Management:

This will entail the Support needed for Transition Planning. It helps coordinate resources when a major Release is due. The plan helps to keep the process within the planned estimates and time. The check on the cost helps one to stick to the predicted cost.

Application Development:

This is involved with the process that ensures availability of applications needed for the IT process. Many of these will involve products from IT vendors that require customization. Others will involve maintenance of custom applications.

Release and Deployment Manager:

This will help you move and test releases in a live environment. Release Management mainly ensures that the live environment does not suffer damage. It also makes sure that the proper components are released.

Service Validation and Testing:

Here you have the verification that the IT service provider aptly supports the new service. The customer expectation forms the base for the validation of the services that arise from new Releases.

Service Asset and Configuration Management:

Here an app check is maintained on Configuration items to ensure that it is delivering the right service. Information is also maintained on their relationships.

Knowledge Management:

In this process, you will see how knowledge is gathered and shared within the organization. This storing process helps improve the efficiency and avoids the need to rediscover knowledge.

RELEASE POLICY

Release Recognition: This will consist of the naming procedure. There may be special numbering present too.

Necessary Conditions: The primary condition for the Release is that it includes the DML.

Levels of Release: This format is followed for all levels of Release. So, include the information in major and minor releases. This is the format for the emergency releases too.

Frequency: What one may expect

Necessary documentation: The needed papers and planning

Deployment of Minor Release: This will use the Minor Change Deployment Process, which is simple. The documentation will take place in Change Records alongside Release Records.

Full Documentation: Full documentation is required when the deployment is a Major Release. A formal project must be set up for this.

Emergency Release: When it is a case of deploying Emergency Release, ECAB must give its authorization. The documentation is carried by Major Incident Team.

Definition of Level of Release

1. Procedure including guidelines and approaches that are used when transiting Changes into Releases.

2. Responsibilities in various roles at different levels of the Management Process for the Deployment and Release. Each stage has a different entry/exit criterion. In addition, the roles might be suitably altered to fit special situations.

3. Guidelines Related to Release Deployment for Different Approaches: This section outlines when one should use a certain type of approach for deployment. This preferred option is of three types:
   3.1. Push--Pull type
   3.2. Phased type against Big-Bang type
   3.3. Manual as opposed to automatic deployment

Release Deployment Constraints

The SLAs and OLAs will give you particulars of the availability targets. You will also have specifications of the maintenance windows when the service might be unobtainable. This will serve as the standard windows for deployment of service unless an Emergency Deployment is needed. Through the use of the Release Management, you can develop constraints for Release Deployment from those constraints that are service-specific. This way you can work the system and applications along with other components needed to keep the service running. The format will be like this:

1. Deployment constraints that are specific to the service: This is given in the SLA and OLA
    1.1. Service A
        1.1.1. Depending on what type of Release it is, the frequency that is to be adopted
        1.1.2. Constraints relating to release windows
    1.2. Service B...
    1.3. Support mechanism that includes the components, applications and system and Constraints related to Release Deployment
        1.3.1. System A
        1.3.2. Depending on what type of Release it is, the frequency that is to be adopted
        1.3.3. Constraints relating to release windows
    1.4. Preferred Mechanisms: The preference of operating systems and devices according to the site and the available facilities.

Request for Change (RFC)

When a change is awaiting implementation, a formal request is needed. Change Management handles this Request for Change (RFC) when the change is non-standard. Small or minor changes that are standard do not require submission to the Change Management lifecycle. The Change Owner backs all these changes and uses the budget for implementing the changes. In this aspect, the RFC initiator is similar to the Change Owner. Most of the changes come under the roles within the Service Management. These would include the Capacity Manager and the Problem Manager. The IT management will handle those that are not covered.

The amount of change required will be reflected in the amount of detail that is needed. Documentation of the details is made. In the process of implementing the changes, the role of the RFC becomes a Project Charter. It leads on to the Change Record. All information needed to approve the change is contained in this. Typically, it will have all this information given below:

1. Submission Date

2. Unique ID

3. Reference to Change Proposal (If there is a Change Proposal submitted earlier)

4. Name of Change Owner

5. RFC Initiator

6. Proposed Priority of Change -- Low, Normal, High, Emergency Change

7. Details of the Requested Change

8. Summary Details

9. Business Case

10. Cost of all the processes involved in the change

11. Reason for the change to become needed

12. Benefits accruing from this change

13. References to earlier incidents

14. Consequences of incorporating the change
    14.1. Affected area in business that will affect the client side due to the change
    14.2. IT Infrastructure Components that will be impacted by the proposed change
    14.3. Services that the change will influence
    14.4. Information on any new technology being introduced by the change

15. Risks
    15.1. Risks that are already identified
    15.2. Measures to counter these risks
    15.3. Back out plan if implementation fails

16. Time for implementation of Plan

17. List of Resources Needed for Implementing Plan

18. Personnel required for implementation with reference to infrastructure

19. Cost list with details of items when change is big

20. Amount of work for the personnel doing the change

21. Budget: Here you will see the statement whether approval has been given for the change or not

22. Design papers and further documents: Needed to modify the service

23. Approval/Rejection Details
    23.1. The person who approves the change: This may be the Change Manager in most cases and the CAB or the ECAB if so required.
    23.2.   Priority that has been assigned to the case by the Change Management
    23.3.   When the case is rejected, the reasons for the same
    23.4.   Date
    23.5.   Reviews on the change

24. Restrictions

Configuration Management Systems/Databases (CMS/CMDB)

Configuration Management Database is contained in the Configuration Management System, which is the set of files relating to data and tools used in configuring data pertinent to the relationships. There may be more than one CMDB in a CMS. Depending on what assets are present in the service, the Configuration model is developed and that forms the basis for the structure. Information is stored through Configuration Items (CIs) under the Configuration Management. These CIs are of different types. CMS is used in IT infrastructure and services. Sometimes, it also finds use in project documentation, employee's database, suppliers list, and policies. Let us see this one by one.

Different kinds of CI and it relationship to Configuration Models: The Configuration Model defines the CMS Structure as already explained. This will exist as data models or document sets. There are instances when it may in the form of a tabular data. Thus, the defined structural aspects of the

CMS are:

1. CI types/subtypes: In CMS, the different types are represented in the tree structure format.
   1.1. Main Type (Staff, Hardware, Software...)
       1.1.1.Subtype (Printer, Supervisor, Server...)
       1.1.2. Further subtypes (Office use, Level 2 staff only...)

2. Status Value: As per the lifecycle of the CI, the allowed status value.

3. Properties: This will list all the properties for each of the subtypes present.

4. Authorities and Control
   4.1. Owner of the CI type
   4.2. Policy and guideline that are applicable
   4.3. Authority: CMS along with its subsystems will have access rights. This is required by the person to access and modify, delete or authorize any CI.

5. Requirements for verification, reporting and auditing
   5.1. Policies, Guidelines, and Controls: As applicable, those mechanisms, controls and procedures that allow only authorized people to modify CIs, or apply changes to CIs, so that consistency is maintained in configuration data.
   5.2. CI Relationships: This will be given in terms of these phrases -- Uses, Component of, New Version of...

6. The configuration

IV) ITIL Service Operation Template

This checklist will ensure effective, efficient and timely delivery of services. This will include resolution of failures in the service, updating and carrying out requests from users, attending to operational tasks in a routine manner and finding solutions to problems. It comprises of the following types of duties:

1. Incident Management: This helps restore service in a quick fashion to users; it helps keep the lifecycle of incidents moving always.

2. Event Management: Monitoring services and CIs and classify events so that the correct decision can be taken.

3. Access Management: This helps authorized users to avail of the services and prevents people without authority to use the system. Security Management information will provide the policies that are applicable. Users also refer to this as Identity Management or Rights Management.

4. IT Operations Control: This portion of the Service Operation Template handles all the IT Operations and its interactions with the underlying infrastructure. It helps conduct routine IT operations and does backup and scheduling operations. It does routine management and helps print outputs.

5. Problem Management: Here you will have the lifecycle of problems. You will work here to minimize the impact of incidents and also study how and when these take place. Records and user information is collected to predict

trends that make incidents unavoidable. This part is known as the Proactive Problem Management.

6. Request Fulfillment: These consist of minor requests like someone asking for information which can be complied with in a standard way. These Service Requests are routine.

7. Technical Management: This helps to support the management by providing technical expertise.

8. Application Management: Governs applications all the way in completing their life cycles.

9. Facilities Management: This is useful in maintaining the physical environment of the infrastructure. Cooling and environmental monitoring are two examples of this type.

The three main checklists in the Service Operation Template are these:

INCIDENT RECORD

This will document an incident from incidence to resolution and all the relevant details. Any unplanned disruption in IT services is termed as an incident. Also, those conditions or situations that could lead to interruption of services are considered an incident. In the normal course, an Incident Record will have all the information given below:

1.1. Time of incident:

1.2. Date:

1.3. Unique ID: This is allocated automatically by the system

1.4. Caller or User Data: Contact information of caller

1.5. Agent monitoring the call: As applicable
1.5.1. Notification Method: The internet, telephone, or mail

1.6. Affected Users, Areas, Businesses

1.7. Description of features of incident

1.8. Method of Call-back

1.9. Relationship to CIs: List of links to CIs damaged by the incident

1.10. Incident Priority: This is determined by the following components:
1.10.1.   Priority -- High, Medium, Low.

1.11. Urgency -- Available time until the problem is resolved

1.12. Major Incident Flag: Yes, or No.

1.13. The severity of Impact: How badly the incident affects the IT infrastructure.

1.14. Affected Services

1.15. Links to Problem Records

1.15.1.   Links to related incidents Records: If any incidents that are outstanding exist that can point to the occurrence of this incident.

1.16. Incident category: This is part of a category tree where the incident is recorded. The relationship between incidents and problems is harmonized to arrive at the best course of action.
1.16.1.   Hardware Error
1.16.1.1.   Server Number 1
1.16.1.1.1.   Name of Component P
1.16.1.1.1.1. Shows the sign A
1.16.1.1.1.2. Shows the sign B
1.16.1.1.1.3. .....
1.16.1.1.2.   Name of Component Q
1.16.1.1.2.1. Shows the sign A
1.16.1.1.2.2......
1.16.1.2.   Server Number 2
1.16.1.3.   Server Number 3....
1.16.2.   Software Error
1.16.2.1.   Error in System A
1.16.2.2.   Error in System B
1.16.3.   Network Error
1.16.4.   .....

1.17. Activity Resolution history: The service desk will maintain a log of steps that show how the incident was resolved. In some incidents, Tasks will be assigned to the incidents. This will have properties such as Name, Owner, Description, Priority and so on. The activity log and status of history will be independently maintained.
1.17.1.   Incident Status change history:
1.17.2.   Time

1.17.3. Date

1.17.4. Reason why there is a change in status

1.17.5. Responsible person

1.17.6. Status of new incident

1.18. Closure data:

1.18.1. Closure categories (Incident category, revised product...)

1.18.2. Resolution Type (Workaround, root cause elimination...)

1.18.3. Problems Raised (Likelihood of problem reoccurring, steps for the same)

1.19. Customer Feedback (When the problem is solved from the point of view of the customer)

INCIDENT PRIORITIZATION GUIDE

This helps us set the right priority for incidents. Since this priority will help determine the escalation value of an incident, setting the correct value is imperative. Priority can be determined by assessing two factors -- urgency and impact. Urgency refers to the time within which the solution must be given. Impact refers to the amount of damage that the incident does.

Incident Urgency

This kind of classification is arbitrary in the sense different organizations will require and use various classifications. In its basic form this will be like this:

LOW -- Time sensitive work is not among the work not completed; marginal increase only of damage over time.

MEDIUM -- One VIP user has been affected; causes a considerable increase of damage over time.

HIGH -- Several VIP Users are affected; time-sensitive work is left incomplete by staff, damage caused increases rapidly, prevent a minor incident from becoming a major incident through prompt action.

Incident Impact

LOW -- Only a low number of people are affected, they are able to deliver the work by putting in an extra effort. Only a minimum number of customers are affected and that too not too badly. Damage to reputation is minimal and costs of damage are less than $1,000 (say, minimal)

MEDIUM -- A moderate number of working crew have been affected and are not able to function properly. The number of customers who are suffering is moderate, not too many, though. Impact moneywise is likely to be greater than $1,000 but less than $10,000. Damage to business is likely to be moderate.

HIGH -- A great number of the working crew have suffered from the incident. The number of customers who suffered this impact is great. The impact moneywise is likely to exceed $10,000. Damage to the reputation of the business is enormous.

Priority Class of Incident

Priority is derived from both the urgency and impact.

We draw the matrix using Impact on one side and Urgency

on the other.

IMPACT versus URGENCY

----

xxx	HIGH	MEDIUM	LOW
HIGH	1	2	3
MEDIUM	2	3	4
LOW	3	4	5

Then we get the following table:

PRIORITY CODE DESCRIPTION TARGET RESPONSE TIME TARGET RESOLUTION TIME

-------------------------- 1 Critical

	Immediate	1 hour	
2	High	10 Minutes	4 hours
3	Medium	1 hour	8 hours
4	Low	4 hours	24 hours
5	Very Low	1 Day	1 Week

Circumstances that show it to be a major incident

This is handled by the Major Incidents Handling Process by the Major Incident Team.

Indicators of Major Incidents: Major incidents should be identified through a ready indicator system. Nevertheless, the first indicators will be given by the priority indicators as given above.

Examples 1: Certain business-critical infrastructure components remain unavailable and recovery times are exceedingly long. Here, the term 'certain' could be referring to 'number of' or 'one'. The item needed could be workforce or applications.

Example 2: Certain Vital Business Functions are affected. Restoration time is unknown. Since the time required to reach full operational status remains undefined, the incident falls into the bracket of a major incident.

Identification Process: One has to toe the line of caution when trying to identify a major incident. The 1st level support team undoubtedly develops a 'sixth sense' that tells it which ones qualify as major incidents.

Examples:

One may consider the following examples to develop a better understanding of how to go about the identification process.

- Several servers in the network develop virus infestation simultaneously.

- Prior to a big public showing (say the premier of a movie), the website shuts down leading to a massive public outcry.

- Network communication link is disrupted leading to 'blackouts' in wide parts of the city.

- Database of a big shopping site has become corrupted.

Key Characteristics: The major incidents will all have some common characteristics. These are as follows:

- Cost of the incident will be heavy (both short and long term) for the customer and the service provider

- Amount of time and effort will be great leading to breaching of agreed resolution time targets

- Several key customers or a large number of customers will remain unable to use the services

- Reputation of the service provider suffers heavily

The Major incident could sometimes be classified as High Priority Incident or Critical Incident.

PROBLEM RECORD

From detection to closure, the Problem Record will make note of all the details of a problem. Contents of the Problem Record will consist of the following material:

1. Detection Time

2. Detection Date

3. Problem Owner

4. Unique ID: This is normally allocated automatically by the system.

5. Affected Services

6. Affected Business and Areas

7. Description of Signs

8. Relation to Cis

9. Priority of the Problem: To identify the priority, we need to consider the following factors:
   9.1. Priority
   9.2. Impact
   9.3. Urgency

10. Problem Category
    10.1. Hardware Error
        10.1.1.   Server Number 1
            10.1.1.1.   Name of Component P
                10.1.1.1.1. Shows the sign A
                10.1.1.1.2. Shows the sign B
                10.1.1.1.3. .....
            10.1.1.2.   Name of Component Q
                10.1.1.2.1. Shows the sign A
                10.1.1.2.2. .....
        10.1.2.   Server Number 2
        10.1.3.   Server Number 3....
    10.2.   Software Error
        10.2.1.   Error in System A
        10.2.2.   Error in System B
    10.3.   Network Error
    10.4.   .....

11. Connection to Related Workarounds and Identified Errors -- If any links exist to identified errors that have similarity or lead to the present error.

12. Connection to Identified Incident Records: If links to previous incidents exist that lead to or are similar to this incident.

13. Connection to Related Problem Records: If links to previous incidents exist that lead to or are similar to this incident.

14. Links to RFCs

15. Problem Status Change History
    15.1. Time
    15.2. Date
    15.3. Reason why there is a change in status
    15.4. Responsible person
    15.5. Status of new incident
16. Activity Log

    16.1. This will consist of a series of steps taken to resolve the incident. However, in some cases, a Task will also be assigned to the incident. This will have its own characteristics like Owner, Description, Name...

V) ITIL Service CSI Template

Learning the Processes

As per the ISO 2000 directive, the policy of continual improvement based on past experiences forms the crux of the CSI Template. This checklist 'learns' from mistakes made in the past to keep the future increments on the positive side. The main processes of the ITIL CSI stage are as follows:

Service Review: The aim of this process is to make

reviews of business services alongside those services within the infrastructure regularly. By doing this, one can improve the quality and reduce costs wherever applicable.

Process Evaluation: To identify those spots within the framework where process metrics are lacking. This process drives evaluation techniques and benchmarking, reviews and maturity assessments throughout the framework.

CSI Initiatives monitoring process: The aim in this process would be to identify the CSI initiatives that you have put in place and verify the progress in each case. It also incorporates corrective measures where and when required.

CSI Initiatives Definitions: These initiatives will help improve processes and thereby augment the quality of the services. Process evaluation and review of service help to define these initiatives. These could be internal, meaning that the service provider requires them to improve the service or it could be related to the customer-side meaning that it will benefit the customer.

CSI Register (Service Improvement Plan -- SIP)

The main checklists in the ITIL CSI Service Template are given below:

Improvement opportunities are managed and recorded for the entirety of the lifecycle in the CSI Register. Continuous Service Improvement will usually trigger additions or alterations to the CSI Register. Improvement Initiatives can be of two types:

1. Initiatives that the service provider undertakes to make

improvements to service or applications.

2. Those that have to be approved by the customer so that they get better service such as when the service levels are no longer adequate.

The CSI Register will comprise of these contents:

- Initiative owner: This will be the person responsible for the initiative, usually having a role in the Service Management. For instance, it could be the Availability Manager or the Capacity Manager. In some cases, the Service Owners and Process Owners might initiate the move. The Service Level Manager will always be knowledgeable about such things.

- Person who handles the process

- Service Owner

- Process Owner

- Name of the service or process

- Description of the initiative

- Approval (usually from the senior management)

- Priority

- Business Case

- Price Calculation

- Result expected from the initiative

- Desired result

- Evaluation Source

- Timetable for the Implementation

- Person who takes charge

- Details of work bundle that need to be fulfilled

- Date for completing work

- Key deliverables

- Status at present

Service Review Report

Results and findings of a Service Review are presented in this report. Based on this, improvement initiatives will be defined. The contents of the Service Review Report will be as follows:

1. Time of review

2. Date of Review

3. Name of the IT Service being reviewed

4. Persons who attended the Service Review Meeting

4.1. Service provider spokesperson

4.2. Business/User spokesperson

5. Person in charge

6. Time interval covered by the review

7. Service levels -- List of approved compared to attained levels

8. Customer Satisfaction: This is from the point of view of the customer. This helps one to mitigate any difference of opinion. This will take the nature of either of the two given below:

8.1. Accolades

8.2. Grievances

9. Report on Unusual Happenings

10. Scope for Refinement: This identifies those areas that will provide better results if you make some changes to it.

11. IT perspective

11.1. Cost improvement: This is achieved either through the use of new technology and devices. Influencing demand for service will help too. Most effective methods will be optimizing the service.

11.2. Identify the correct areas: The right areas where improvement is needed is identified and earmarked.

12. Customer Perspective

12.1. Anticipating changes in service consumption: This must cover the short term, medium term and long term periods.

12.2.New requirements in functionality that arise from strategy changes or variations in business processes.

12.3.Needed modifications for the short term: This arises from difficulties that are current.

13. Altered Service Level Targets due to changes in priorities or risk perception.

14. Altered service level reporting due to changes in requirements.

Chapter 15: Lean Development

Lean software development (LSD) comes originally from a book written by Mary and Tom Poppendieck where they present Lean principles with modifications. They also give 22 tools and make comparisons to Agile practices.

Lean Principles

These seven principles summarize the principles of this software development method.

1. Satisfy Customer Needs Fast

2. Abolish Waste

3. Intensify Wisdom

4. Delay Decisions for Getting Facts

5. Whole Working System

6. Inbuilt Integrity Is Must

7. Team Works Independently

Customers Need Their Products Today

Survival, from the point of view of the customer, depends not on being strong and big, but on being quick. Time makes the difference that translates into money. To develop good products that are free from defects, feedback is essential. This must be obtained within a short span of time. Making each iteration shorter leads to faster cycles. This helps you deliver quality goods in a shorter time interval.

When applied to software development, the production principle of Just-In-Time changes according to the specific needs and environment in which it unwraps. For instance, if the team was presented with a much-desired result, the entire process will be broken into small pieces. These specific bits form the iteration that is represented as story or picture cards. The developing team will come up with an estimate for each card. The entire system thus translates into a self-pulling-system.

Progress is monitored through the daily morning meetings where everyone has some information for all the others. He or she will tell what they did during the course of the day and what they have in mind for the next day. This will provide input for other team members who are doing tasks related this work being discussed. This is the stand-up meeting where everyone learns about the problems. It enables several teams to come up with solutions. The best solution is chosen (those that do not solve the problem are discarded then and there, eliminating waste of time and effort).

Recognize waste and eliminate it

Anything that does not improve on the present value of the product being developed is a waste. We can see this waste in different ways. The apt way to do this is through Value Stream Mapping. In this method, the mapping team does the planning and preparation for the mapping of the flow process. The entire resources and service are taken through from the start of the process, which is the present state, to the future state. All unnecessary material, processes, and services are removed. The new map is then put into practice.

Work not needed for obtaining the final product is a waste. So, is work that is not completed (it will not help fulfill the final product). Anything that can be removed without affecting the process of production of the service is also a waste. Features and processes that are not required are removed. Use of defective or lower quality processing techniques or material is a waste. You will simply have to discard them as otherwise you might have to do the entire thing again.

Waiting time in between your regular working time is a waste. This will include waiting for managerial instructions and waiting for other processes to finish. Find ways to work without these encumbrances. Another point of wastage is the paperwork and use of another worker in the middle of a work. Paperwork leads to unnecessary waste of time. There is endless discussion and the conclusion is reached which they would have anyway without the paper. If you change a worker during the work, the new worker has to 'learn' the starting and ending point of the work first. Next, there are anomalies in the quality of the work between the two. This will result in unnecessary time consumption -- meaning it is a waste.

Codes that are not carried forward to fulfillment are a waste. Since, this partial code will not benefit the final product, the time, and energy spent on it will become waste. Waste can also take the form of moving around for completion of the work. The movement is a waste. If you eliminate this movement, you will get work done faster without waste of time and energy.

Learning Is Important

For efficiency when writing code, the learning process is essential. The feedback is studied and the integration is done based on these results. This makes the code more appropriate to the working situation.

Another approach is to increase the types of codes you try with the work increment. Integration testing and refactoring form a vital part of this process. The domain problems become more apparent to both the developers and the customer side representatives. This clarifies the needs of the customer and helps uncover aspects of the solution that had so far eluded them. This is the way learning process is integrated into the software development.

Do Not Make Hasty Decisions

When you wait, there is a possibility that a better solution will be presented. If you hurry up with the step, then you will need to repeat the step since the answer might not have that much accuracy. In the place of one iteration, if you do two iterations, then the answer comes closer to perfection. By delaying the process of selection, you get more choices that will help the customer derive more benefit.

This kind of delaying will help offset the costs too. Expensive iterations can be avoided clearing the way for more adaptations and better choices of the solution. Of course, this does not mean that you wait during the lifecycle and delay the running of the process. It only means that when it is time to make the decision, you must wait and not jump to any result blindly.

See the whole thing clearly

For the full functioning of the software, one must consider more than one aspect, including the sum of the individual components that contributed to the solution. Secondly, the interactions of these components will help move towards the solution. When you have a large project to work on, there are more vendors who do the software development. This expands the picture so that it becomes difficult to see everything at once. For ensuring the smoothness in process for different interacting components, enough testing and iterations must be carried out. Only then, the entire thing will become clear. This type of 'common sense' approach helps you get success in a short time in Lean development.

Integrity Is Inbuilt

Customers have a better working sense of the system when they are able to interact with the common approach that outlines the values and principles to adopt. This integrity helps the user develop an intuitive feel for the way they must use the solution. This is done by making small pieces of the entire approach and working on these small bits one at a time. The next solution in the iterative approach is built on the previous solution. This makes the final solution as the sum of all the intermittent solutions. If the customer is held up at any point, he or she is able to see the relationship to the final solution in an intuitive manner.

Team Has Full Power to Do Its Work

Using an inversion principle, the entire team listens to the other team members. Developers increase their interaction with Managers and the workers are able to implement more detail in their work. The traditional approach to work forms the first tier of operations while the successive iterations are based on the personal output they receive in the course of completing this work. This leads to a better understanding of the overall work.

In case there is a problem at some point and a hitch develops, the piece of work is reexamined at the completion of the iteration. If it is found to be unsuitable for further work, it is discarded and another solution is deployed. In all matters, the team members do their own work. Nobody tells them to 'do this' or 'do that'. Individual problems are brought forward at the team meetings. The solutions are discussed with the entire team and people who have solutions put their suggestions to those who want it.

By adopting this approach, the commitment of the worker to his or her work achieves fullness. This kind of dedication will make the work to achieve integrity. The reality that can be achieved becomes obvious. Instead of 'talking' about big things, the team, in reality, achieves big things.

Tools That Help Us Learn and Use Lean Easily

Improving Visibility

Having a better view of the materials by cleaning up the approach and systems helps us recognize waste. As explained above, eliminating waste is a key concept of Lean technique. The types of waste are explained in detail below.

Identify waste as those steps in the work process that do not add value. Adopting this kind of rigid approach of not accepting work without value is difficult to implement but a necessary part of the Lean process. Once you have identified those processes that do not add value, you eliminate them.

Next, you come to the work that you are doing after eliminating the unnecessary work. Here again, you can make the subdivision as work that adds value and those items of the work process that is needed but does not add value. When you examine the needed-to-be done work, you get another pure waste class.

This process of learning to see helps you understand the waste steps in the work process. To generalize, these following resources will be wasted.

Standby time: Since the work time comprises of every hour you spend on the work site, any time that you spend not doing work will be waste. The time you wait for material to arrive, for the management to approve the start of your work or the tool set to be delivered will add up to the overall picture as a waste. It is important, therefore, to identify areas in the workplace where you have 'waiting' and eliminate such occurrences.

Moving during work: When a person has to move during the work, it reduces his efficiency. First, in terms of energy expended, there is a segment of the work that is not a 'plus'. This is the moving to get the material, moving to place the material or moving to operate the machine. By marking these spots and eliminating the movement, you will reduce waste in energy and improve working efficiency.

Over listing of requirements: When making the inventory, people frequently list items that they will not use. The idea of being prepared for the eventuality makes them do this. This results in many items that they end up not using. This kind of waste might come from being over cautious or from lack of application. The workers may not have the capability to work with the tools provided. Or the technology might be too advanced for their level of work. This results in underutilization of the processes and tools. First, identify the tools and processes that are not used and then remove them from the framework.

Unnecessary items: When items in the inventory, either finished goods, work-in-progress or raw material, have not produced any useful output in terms of money or services, they are unnecessary items. One must make the effort to identify these materials at the source and eliminate them in the current situation and make an effort to avoid the possibility of such occurrences in the future.

Use of inferior types of material: Choice of low-quality material will result in unwanted wastage. The system will collapse due to the poor quality of workmanship and you have to spend more money on repair work and maintenance. Use only material that has passed the recommended standards of quality. This will also help you finish the work faster because the superior material will have better workability. If you see the low-quality material in use anywhere inform the matter to your superiors.

Overworking: This is bad for two reasons. One, you will spend unnecessarily large amounts of time on the work. Two you will not achieve the required standard of workmanship. You can see this problem from two perspectives.

Too much work done on the piece: Overworking with one single piece will diminish the value of the piece. It will lead to errors and in most cases you have to repeat the work.

Too many pieces are produced: If you produce too many pieces, the market value will diminish. You have to wait until the market is ready to buy up your pieces. This means you will not produce in the meantime. This will lead to further loss. One way to avoid this is to use the Kanban system explained below.

Kanban Principles

This scheduling system was used predominantly in Japan but is now being adopted the world over. The simplicity of use combined with its effectiveness makes this a good tool for controlling the supply chain. Through the use of Kanban, you can achieve JIT.

All work-in-progress items in the inventory can have their upper limit set through Kanban. You can easily establish problem areas as well as places where there is deficit or overloading. The rate of delivery is controlled by the demand rate and the signal is sent through the framework that is seen by the customer, the supplier and the management.

You can liken the process to that of a mall, where the just-in-time principle holds good. The goods are given to the customer when they require it. For this reason, the customer tends to buy just what he needs. The demand is constant at the time of study and so there is always just enough to give the customers just what they want.

In Kanban, the owner studies the preceding processes. This becomes his mall. He is the customer and he 'takes' just what he needs -- meaning the supply for the next step in the production process. As and when this is consumed he signals the process to produce one more item. This keeps the wheels turning and the supply constant. But the supply never exceeds the demand because of the constant monitoring.

According to that Toyota Company that adopted this system for its company, the Kanban that the earlier process shows will be used by the later processes. All processes will use a Kanban. The sensitivity of the system increase when the number of Kanban is reduced. The Japanese never uses defective products. You can easily visualize the system of operation in a factory where the parts are supplied from some external point (supplier). The factory floor will signal its needs with a Kanban. The cart that it has will be used for assembly. Once this is depleted, it will send the empty cart to the factory store. The store will send a full cart back with another Kanban card.

The empty cart now at the factory store will be sent to the supplier. The supplier will send the new full cart back to the factory store. The factory never operates with excess carts. It has maximum one spare cart and this way the supply is never in excess of demand.

Queueing Theory

Waiting lines are important everywhere especially on the factory floor or in a supply chain. Study of mathematical models of these queues is named as 'Queueing Theory'. The aim is to decrease the time spent on the line as well as to decrease the number of items or people in the line.

Agner Erlang first researched this idea. It has since grown to find use extensively in production management and design of management processes. He denoted the queueing process using the M/D/k symbols. This meant that there were M signals arriving at a node or in the queue. D denotes the amount of work that needed to be done. The number of available servers was denoted by k. Thus, k could take the values 1,2...

The scheduling policy for these queues could be fashioned according to one of the following:

- *First in -- First out*: This refers to the system where the service attends to customers one by one. The customer who is waiting the longest time will be served first.

- *Last in -- First out*: In this system, the person who has been waiting for the shortest time is sent out first.

- *Sharing system*: All customers have an equal opportunity at being served.

Determining Priority

High priority customers will find the service quickest. In this, we have preemptive queues and non-preemptive queues. The preemptive jobs can be interrupted if another job with a higher priority comes up. The non-preemptive jobs will not be and cannot be interrupted. Either way, the work proceeds without any loss of work.

Shortest job first: The job that is taken up is the one with the smallest size.

Preemptive shortest job first: In this case, the job taken up will be one where the size is smallest originally.

Shortest remaining processing time: When a job has the smallest possible requirement for processing, it will be taken up as the next job.

The system available for servicing the customers will vary from place to place.

Just one server: Customers have to line up and wait because there is only one server available.

More than one server: This is a parallel system where people can use many servers.

Tandem queueing facility: In this system, many counters are made available for customers. They can decide at which counter they want their service from at any point in time.

Usually, the customer behavior while waiting in the queue is normal. But, occasionally there is a chance for variations as shown below.

Jockey for the position: When the customer notices faster movement in any one line, they will switch to that one. This way they will get a faster service.

Balking: This tendency is shown when the line is too long and the movement in the line is too slow. The people will hesitate to join that line. They will abandon that line and move over to some other.

Reneging the chance: The people who wait too long will move away without waiting for their turn. This is one way to avoid wasting time and energy when there is lesser choice.

Chapter 16: Theory Of Constraints

This management paradigm views constraints that will be present in any manageable system and then models the system around that weakest link in the system. This means if there is a link that is bound to fail soon within the system, then that will form the focus of the paradigm. It only shows that the weak person will invariably damage the system at the place where they are present.

Eliyahu M. Goldratt proposed this management policy in 1984. The premise of this theory is that three basic parameters will be enough to control any system. These would be:

1. Inventory

2. Operational Expense

3. Throughput

So, this link shows how the money is utilized by an enterprise. The Inventory will be the entire sum the concern has invested to buy material to make goods. The sales output is given by Throughput. The Operational Expense is the amount of money that has been spent in turning the Inventory into Throughput.

FIVE STEPS OF FOCUS

There is always at least one constraint restraining the system at all times. This acts on the goal oriented system and affects its rate. By theory, there can be a situation where throughput is increased limitlessly. But in reality, this would not be possible because we cannot make money limitlessly.

We see we need to send increased work output through the constraint in order to achieve the increased throughput. When the system goal has been defined and there are enough steps to achieve the goal the focus is on these five steps:

1. Make a correct identification of the constraints in the system

2. Elaborate a plan whereby the exploitation of the constraints takes place.

3. Everything in the framework will be subject to these decisions that you made.

4. Raise the level of your system constraints.

5. If the constraint fails to achieve the goal, go back to the first step and begin the work again.

Defining the Constraint

Anything that prevents your system from achieving its goal is a constraint. The occurrence of constraints is inevitable but usually, only one or two core principles will be affected. Depending on where it occurs, we term the constraint as internal or external.

You can see this as the imbalance of the supply and demand existing in the market. When there is too much demand for the product, the system is not up to the mark to give what is demanded. This is an internal constraint. The obvious solution is to increase the output by employing more labor and using more material as and when the market demand is more.

The external failure, therefore, will be the opposite case. This is when the supply is too much and the market is unable to take up all the products that are made. The solution, in this case, would be to open the market up a little more. This could be done by advertising or forming cooperatives that will take up your excess produce.

Internal Constraints Types

We can categorize internal constraints into the following three types:

1. People

2. Policy

3. Equipment

One must have good workmen who have the capacity to deliver quality goods. Secondly, the attitude of the people must be good. If they have hang-ups regarding the work, then the quality will suffer.

To achieve more, the aim of the workers must be aligned in the direction of that of the management. Meaning, if the workers do not like to work on Thursdays when there is a weekly market, the chances of making more money is not achievable. Now, this is the motive of all organizations and this should be at the back of the mind of the workers too.

There has to be sufficiently high-quality equipment for the workers. Working without adequate tools will only result in shoddy work. The returns will suffer as a result. The management must invest in good tools and machines if they wish to get quality results and make more money.

Overcoming the constraint: The term here is 'break the constraint'. It does not refer to a failure of the system. On the contrary, it refers to the point in time when the said constraints fail to act as the limiting factor. The constraint is broken. When this happens, the constraint moves away and occupies another portion of the system.

Use of Buffers

Buffers are helpful for maintaining the integrity of the system and for effective governance of the constraints. Usually, buffers are placed before the dominant constraints so that adequate functioning is maintained at all times. These are actually time buffers. This buys us time to act in case there is a deviation and there is unusual activity.

At times, it may be needed to keep buffers behind the constraint. This is needed since downstream failure will upset the constraint and cause system failure. Buffers thus ensure normal variations in processing time for differing conditions. One may use physical objects as buffers also. The work required by the buffer is enough but not excessive. It helps you get some time. In the same manner, enough space is also ensured after the buffer. This helps in offloading.

The Kanban system ensures that the entire system is operating without a break. If there were a time delay, then the entire framework will have to wait until the breakdown is fixed. All other processes would have to sit around and wait. This is prevented if the buffer is adequate and efficient.

Applying buffers in any system have to remain simple. Most common application is the visual application. The three colors red, green and yellow are used to indicate the status of the buffer. The first red indicates "Action needed". The second one, green shows "Everything is fine". And the third one yellow will indicate "Caution".

Plant types in Theory of Constraints

In this theory, we have four types of plants. We classify them according to the shape or functionality of their assembly or manufacturing line.

1. I-plant: Here there is no crossing of the lines. The assembly proceeds in straight lines without any interaction.

2. A-plant: In this type of assembly, there is a many-to-one convergence. This may be the final point or may form a new starting point for the next stage of the assembly.

3. V-plant: In this assembly, one is sent to many places. For example, this happens when there is more than one product being made with one material. There is a problem of "robbing" in this type of plant. Material meant for this stage is stolen at the point of divergence and proceeds to the next point. Then, it is a big task bringing the work back and redoing it all again.

4. T-plant: Here the work is more or less like that of an I-plant. After the linear movement, the material is then moved on a many-to-many basis. T-plants have big problems with synchronization.

Conclusion

From the many variants of Agile, users make the selection of the process most suitable to their work atmosphere. One methodology is not superior to the next one. Users of Management Processes choose from the many variants of Agile by studying the work atmosphere. Scrum, Kanban, DSDM Atern, RUP & AUP, Xtreme Programming and Lean are all remarkably alike but each of them possesses certain qualities that suit different work environments.

DSDM has many customary methodologies used in management such as the use of plans, a project manager, and a project board. Many companies that are currently using PRINCE2 or such similar technologies will be able to easily adapt to DSDM. This generic quality of DSDM is preferable to many.

For people who have IT projects, the choice of the methodology will be Scrum. Scrum has less documentation and is, therefore, lightweight. It has been extremely successful though it cannot be adapted so easily to traditional working methods.

By studying the differences existing between the different methodologies, users can arrive at the best one for their project.

References and Attributes

The Scrum Guide™ The Definitive Guide to Scrum: The Rules of the Game – Developed and sustained by Ken Schwaber and Jeff Sutherland

©2014 Scrum.Org and ScrumInc.

Offered for license under the Attribution Share-Alike license of Creative Commons, accessible at http://creativecommons.org/licenses/by-sa/4.0/legalcode and also described in summary form at http://creativecommons.org/licenses/by-sa/4.0/. By utilizing this Scrum Guide you acknowledge and agree that you have read and agree to be bound by the terms of the Attribution Share-Alike license of Creative Commons.

http://www.techrepublic.com/blog/tech-decision-maker/adaptive-project-framework-a-new-level-of-Agile-development/

http://www.projecttimes.com/articles/adaptive-project-management.html

Tutorialspoint.com/Agile Project Management

http://www.allaboutAgile.com/what-is-Agile-10-key-principles/ Kelly Walters, 101 ways: All About Agile, 10 February 2007, *10 Key Principles of Agile Development*

https://en.wikipedia.org/wiki/Dynamic_systems_development_method

http://www.codeproject.com/Articles/5097/What-Is-DSDM

http://www.tutorialspoint.com/scrum/scrum_overview.htm

https://www.dsdm.org/what-is-dsdm

https://en.wikipedia.org/wiki/Dynamic_systems_developm
ent_method

http://www.codeproject.com/Articles/5097/What-Is-DSDM

http://www.tutorialspoint.com/scrum/scrum_overview.htm

https://www.axelos.com/Corporate/media/Files/Misc%20Q
ualification%20Docs/ITIL_Value_Proposition-(1).pdf
(Terms of Use)

https://www.axelos.com/policies/legal/permitted-use-of-
white-papers-and-case-studies

http://www.tutorialspoint.com//itil/itil_quick_guide.htm

http://wiki.en.it-processmaps.com/index.php/ITIL_Roles

http://wiki.en.it-processmaps.com/index.php/ITIL-
Checklists

http://wiki.en.it-processmaps.com/index.php/Main_Page

http://wiki.en.it-processmaps.com/index.php/ITIL-
Checklists

http://wiki.en.it-
processmaps.com/index.php/Checklist_Service_Portfolio

http://wiki.en.it-processmaps.com/index.php/Checklist_SLA_OLA

http://wiki.en.it-processmaps.com/index.php/ITIL-Checklists

https://en.wikipedia.org/wiki/Kanban

https://en.wikipedia.org/wiki/Queueing_theory

http://wiki.en.it-processmaps.com/index.php/Checklist_Financial_Analysis

Made in the USA
San Bernardino, CA
12 June 2017